ARE YOU THERE, VODKA? IT'S ME, CHELSEA

CHELSEA HANDLER

SSE

SIMON SPOTLIGHT ENTERTAINMENT

New York London Toronto Sydney

Names and identifying characteristics have been changed.

SIMON SPOTLIGHT ENTERTAINMENT
An imprint of Simon & Schuster
1230 Avenue of the Americas
New York, New York 10020

First Simon Spotlight Entertainment trade paperback edition December 2009

For information about special discounts for bulk purchases, please contact Simon & Schuster Special Sales at 1-800-456-6789 or business@simonandschuster.com.

Designed by Gabe Levine

Manufactured in the United States of America

10 9 8

Library of Congress Cataloging-in-Publication Data
Handler, Chelsea.
Are you there, vodka? It's me, Chelsea / by Chelsea Handler.—1st ed.
p. cm.
1. Man-woman relationships. 2. Sex. I. Title.
HQ801.H3193 2008
306.7092—dc22
2007039729

ISBN 978-1-4169-5412-5
ISBN 978-1-4165-9636-3 (pbk)
ISBN 978-1-4169-5915-1 (ebook)

To my mother.

I love you, chunky monkey.

Contents

CHAPTER ONE
Blacklisted

I was nine years old and walking myself to school one morning when I heard the unfamiliar sound of a prepubescent boy calling my name. I had heard my name spoken out loud by males before, but it was most often by one of my brothers, my father, or a teacher, and it was usually followed up with a shot to the side of the head.

I turned around and spotted Jason Safirstein. Jason was an adorable fifth-grader with an amazing lower body who lived down the street from me. I had never walked to school, had a conversation with, or even so much as made eye contact with Jason before. After lifting up one of my earmuffs to make sure I had heard him correctly, I nervously attempted to release my wedgie while waiting for him to catch up. (A futile effort, as it turned out, when wearing two mittens the size of car batteries.)

"I heard you were going to be in a movie with Goldie Hawn," he said to me, out of breath.

Shit. I had worried something like this was going to happen. The day before, I had forgotten my language arts homework, and when the teacher singled me out in front of the entire class to find out where it was, I told her that I had been in three straight nights of meetings with Goldie Hawn and Kurt Russell, negotiating my contract to play Goldie Hawn's daughter in the sequel to *Private Benjamin*.

The fact that no sequel to *Private Benjamin* was in the works, or that a third-grader wouldn't be negotiating her own contract with the star of the movie and her live-in lover, hadn't dawned on me.

"Yeah, well, that was kind of a lie," I mumbled, recovering my left mitten from in between my butt cheeks.

"What?" he asked, astounded. "You lied? Everyone has been talking about it. Everyone thinks it's so cool."

"Really?" I asked, quickly changing my tune, realizing the magnitude of what had happened. It occurred to me that this was the perfect opportunity to get some of the respect I believed had been denied me, due to my father dropping me off in front of the school in a 1967 banana yellow Yugo. It was 1984, and my father had no idea of or interest in how damaging his 1967 Yugo had been to my social status. He had driven me to school on a couple of really cold days, and even after I had pleaded with him to drop me off down the street, he was adamant about me not catching a cold.

"Dad," I would tell him over and over again, "the weather has nothing to do with catching a cold. It has to do with your immune system. Please let me walk. Please!"

"Don't be stupid," he would tell me. "That's child abuse."

I wanted my father to know that child abuse was embarrassing your daughter on a regular basis with no clue at all as to the repercussions. Word had spread like wildfire throughout the school about what kind of car my father drove, and before I knew it, the older girls in fifth grade would follow me through the hallways calling me "poor" and "ugly." After a couple of months they upped it from "ugly" to "a dog," and would bark at me anytime they saw me in the hallway.

Our family certainly wasn't poor, but we lived in a town where trust funds, sleepaway camps, and European vacations were abundant, along with Mercedes, Jaguars, and BMWs—a far cry from my world filled with flat tires, missing windshield wipers, and cars with perpetually lit CHECK ENGINE lights.

The idea that showing up at school in a piece of shit jalopy led to me looking like a dog didn't make much sense in my mind. It really irked me that I had to be punished because my father thought he was a used car dealer and insisted on driving us around in the cars that he couldn't sell. I wanted to tell my classmates that I didn't like his cars either, and I certainly didn't like being called a dog. I hadn't had a low opinion of myself before then, but after being called the same nickname for six months straight, you start to look in the mirror and see resemblances between yourself and a German shepherd.

If it had been mild teasing, I think I probably could have handled it. But it was incessant, and started from the moment I got to school until the moment I left. After a while, most of my friends in the third grade would avoid being seen with me in the hallways because they didn't want to be blacklisted too. My best friend, Jodi Sapperman, was the only one who would walk with me to every class and defend me when the fifth-grade girls would come over to our table in the cafeteria and ask if I was eating Alpo for lunch.

"Well, I shouldn't have said 'lie.' That's the wrong word," I told Jason. "I'm having trouble getting the trailer size I want. Goldie's being pretty cool, but Kurt is so mercurial. He doesn't understand why a nine-year-old needs a Jacuzzi and a personal chef," I said nonchalantly, with a wave of my mitten. "These types of things always take time."

"You get your own trailer?" he asked.

"Yeah, you know, your own little house when you're on set. Every actor gets one. There's sooo much downtime in movies, you really need a place to unwind. In my opinion, it's not nearly large enough to live in for three months, but it's my first major role, so I'm willing to settle for a little less than the crème de la crème."

My vast knowledge of movie-making at the age of nine came from spending every free minute watching television, movies, and reading any book about the filming of *The Breakfast Club* I could get my hands on. I think when you grow up in a house surrounded by cars from the previous two decades and parents who insist that ten dollars for a pair of jeans in 1984 is excessive, you have no choice but to immerse yourself in a world where money is no object.

"I didn't even know you were an actress," Jason said. "How did you get the part?"

"It's 'actor'," I said, correcting him. "The thing is, I was in a little Off-Broadway production with Meryl Streep." I took a long pause, allowing him to interrupt.

"Meryl Streep?" he asked. "The one from *Sophie's Choice*?"

"Is there another?" I asked, rolling my eyes at his naivete. "Anyway, she and I really clicked. She recommended me to the director of this movie. That's how Hollywood works—one thing leads to another, blah, blah, blah. But they're having a ton of creative issues, so who knows if it will even go."

"Go where?" he asked.

"If the movie will even be made."

"Oh."

I could tell Jason was disappointed and I didn't want to lose his attention, so I hurried to keep him interested. I had always dreamed of becoming romantically involved with an older man and thought Jason not only had the makings of a wonderful lover, but also of a dedicated father to the two black twins I had planned on adopting from Ethiopia. "I mean, it will go, but it could take months. Maybe you can visit me on set."

"Really?" he asked, his eyes ready to pop out of their sockets.

I had to think of something quick to recant my offer after realizing I would never be able to pull it off, so I quickly added,

"Well, I mean if your parents will let you fly to the Galapagos Islands."

"Who?"

"The Galapagos," I said, trying to come up with a reason they would be shooting the sequel to *Private Benjamin* surrounded by turtles. "They have a ton of rare animals there, so the movie's going to be more of her roughing it in the water with jellyfish and sea horses. It's basically a cross between *Splash* and *Private Benjamin*."

"I loved *Splash*!" Jason screamed. "This is so cool!"

"Darryl's a complete mess," I told him, shaking my head.

"Darryl Hannah?"

"Don't even get me started," I snorted.

Once we arrived at school, I played it cool and left Jason with his mouth agape, as I told him I'd talk to him later and went on my way. It felt great to get attention from him. Even if our star signs didn't end up being sexually compatible, he was cute and popular, and it would definitely not hurt to have him as a friend. He could be the perfect ally to help get the evil fifth-grade girls to show me a little respect.

By lunch, almost every person at school had asked me about the movie. Not only did the fifth-grade girls skip their daily harassment, one of them even said "hi" as she walked by. Not one person had made fun of me or barked at me all day. Before Jodi and I could even sit down to eat lunch, kids were scrambling to come up to my table.

"What's Goldie Hawn like?" one of the other boys in fifth grade asked me.

"Tiny," I told him. "We're practically the same size."

"Really? She seems so much taller in the movies."

"She's like a mom to me. We totally get each other."

Once we had a minute to ourselves, Jodi finally confronted me and said she knew for a fact I hadn't been in a play with Meryl Streep, never mind the Off-Broadway version of *Sesame Street*, which by lunchtime I had cleverly renamed *Sesame Streep*.

"I know, Jodi, but look at it this way: This is the first day in months that I haven't been called a dog or ugly by the fifth-graders, and I'll be honest with you, it feels pretty sweet."

"I know," she said, "but what are you gonna do when they find out you're lying?"

"They'll forget about it," I said, loving the attention. "I'll just tell them it shoots over the summer, and by the time everyone gets back next year, they'll have forgotten. Plus, all the fifth-graders will have gone to middle school by then, so they can suck it."

"Yeah, but what about everybody else?" she asked. "Isn't there a way you could actually get to meet Goldie Hawn and at least get a picture with her?"

"That's a great idea," I told her as I unbuckled my Ms. Pac-Man lunchbox to find a peanut-butter-and-cream-cheese sandwich. "What the hell is this?" I asked, unwrapping it and then slamming it down on the table. "My parents are the worst."

Jodi and I had been friends since kindergarten, so she was used to this kind of mix-up. As sweet and loving as my mother was, she had the organizational skills of a sea lion and could never remember to make me lunch. So every morning I had to tell my father to make it for me. He, in turn, had the culinary skills of a sea lion, and no matter how many times I repeated the phrase "peanut butter and jelly," he always somehow managed to fuck it up.

"Do you want half of my sandwich?" Jodi asked, offering me the other half of her ham and cheese. Had I not kept kosher my entire third-grade year, I would have dove into it headfirst.

"Just forget it," I said, skipping the sandwich and taking a bite out of one of my Ding Dongs.

The day grew more and more insane as well-wishers and new fans were approaching me left and right, prying for information. One first-grader even asked me for my autograph. By the end of the day, not only were we filming in the Galapagos, but Soleil Moon Frye, a.k.a. Punky Brewster, would be playing my sister in the movie. Then I realized that her dark hair and freckles were in stark contrast to my blond hair and blue eyes and quickly made her my stepsister instead.

By the time school let out, everyone who lived in my neighborhood was racing to get one-on-one time with me, and I walked home with eight other children. The great thing about this attention was that it was coming from all the older kids, who I always believed were my core demographic. I always felt older than the kids my age, and I would get so frustrated when the other third-graders showed no interest in trying to help me figure out what really went down during the Nixon administration a decade earlier. I remember having this feeling early on, during my second day of kindergarten. It became apparent to me that all of my classmates had the necessary faculties to play a serious game of Pin the Tail on the Donkey, but had no designs on how to forge a late note from their parents.

I constantly had visions of skipping a grade or two, becoming a trailblazer of sorts, and possibly inventing something along the lines of Cabbage Patch Kid "Plus." Once patented, it would look and feel like a regular Cabbage Patch Kid, but would also be able to help you with chores around the house. It would be able to speak different languages like Spanish and Farsi, and if you poked it in the eye, it would shit out a peanut-butter-and-jelly sandwich on rye.

I walked into my house that cold December day floating on air. "Hi, Mom!" I said as I triumphantly threw my backpack on the ground and skipped into the kitchen.

"Chelsea, sweetie, your father just got off the phone with your principal, Mr. Hiller."

"What kind of meshugas is this, Chelsea?" my father asked, using one of his two favorite Yiddish phrases. "You're shooting a movie with Goldie Hawn and flying to the Galapagos?"

My whole day deflated in a matter of seconds. "Mrs. Schectman was making a big deal about me not doing my homework and the Goldie Hawn story was the only thing I could think of," I told them.

"Well, why didn't you do your homework?" he asked me.

"Because, Dad!" I wailed, bursting into tears and stomping my left foot. "It was the season premiere of *Charles in Charge*! Are you out of your tree?"

"Chelsea, sweetie, you don't have to make up such far-fetched lies," my mother said in her ultracalm tone. "Couldn't you have come up with something a little more reasonable?"

"I know," I told her, defeated, and walked over for a hug. My mother was always a softie, and once I got over to her I knew my father would cease being such an immediate physical threat. "But everyone started to believe it and all the older kids were asking me about it and I got carried away."

"Well," my father said dismissively, "you're just going to have to go back to school tomorrow and tell everyone the truth."

The problem with being the youngest of six children is that my father had me when he was forty-two years old, resulting in what I like to refer to as "severe generational gappage." That, coupled with the fact that he was born without the embarrassment gene, left us little in common. It would have seemed completely appropriate to my father for me to hold a press conference in the school's auditorium the next day, wearing a helmet with a maxipad stuck to my forehead while announcing into a microphone that I'd been a "bad, bad girl, and I've also been known to shit my pants."

"Melvin," my mother said, "that is going to be extremely humiliating."

"Well, she certainly can't go on pretending she's going to be joining the army with some Hollywood hotshot."

"The sequel isn't going to be as much about the army as it will be about sea creatures," I corrected him.

"Chelsea, what are you even talking about?"

"I can't tell the truth. Then the older girls will go back to calling me a dog."

"Listen to me," my father screamed. "We've been over this before. If those girls are going to make fun of you because of the kind of car your father drives, then they're not worth your time anyway."

"That's nice, Dad," I told him. "But it doesn't matter if they're not worth my time or not, it's a lot more pleasant going through the halls at school not getting growled at."

"How many times do we have to tell you that spending money on material things is not important? What is driving around in a Mercedes or a BMW going to teach you?" he asked.

"I dunno," I said, still clinging to my mother. "That I want a Mercedes or a BMW?"

"Chelsea," my father repeated, "you cannot just make up lies."

"You lie all the time," I reminded him, and then ran behind my mother and wrapped my arms around her waist to shield me from any impending wrath. "You tell all the people who call about your cars that they run great, or that they have no leaks, or that they're in mint condition. Half of them need to be jump-started on a daily basis."

"Listen to me, you little mouthpiece. I am the father," he said, heading over in our direction while I buried my face in my mother's ass. "You are nine years old and you are going to have to do what I tell you for the next nine years, whether you like it or not. As long as you're living under this roof. Do you understand me?"

I wanted to tell him that I had no problem looking in the

want ads for an apartment to sublet, but knew the reality of me getting my own place was months away.

"Yes," I said, in order to avoid getting bitch-slapped. "I understand."

"That's enough, Melvin," my mother told him. "Why don't you sit down and I'll make you some porridge."

Even though porridge is a perfectly suitable meal for a bear, I couldn't resist asking my mother if we were having Goldilocks over for dinner. My father was still in earshot as he headed over to the living room couch, where he normally took his three o'clock feeding. It took one look from him to send me airborne in the direction of the stairs, which I took two steps at a time.

Once safely inside my room, I weighed my options. I could either tell the truth to all the kids at school and endure that embarrassment, or go for the more palatable option—enroll myself in a performing-arts boarding school.

Instead, I got out some loose-leaf notebook paper and started a letter to Goldie Hawn:

Dear Goldie,

I am a third-grader from New Jersey and consider myself to be a huge fan of yours as well as a compulsive liar. I made the mistake of mentioning that I would be playing your daughter in the next installment of *Private Benjamin*. (A fine performance if I do say so myself. I have seen a lot of movies, and can pretty much, without a sliver of a doubt, tell you that your range far outweighs the likes of Robert De Niro or, my personal favorite, Don Johnson.)

Anyway, it would be of great help to me if you could either come to my school in New Jersey and pick me up for lunch, or send me a personalized autographed photo that reads:

My Dearest Chelsea,
Working together has been a dream come true.
Love Always,
Goldie (your second mom)

Once I sealed the envelope, I spent three hours trying to get her agent on the phone. The furthest I got was to an operator at William Morris who gave me the address for fan mail. I was convinced that not only would she get the letter, but that, in my estimation, it wouldn't take more than a week for her to respond. I then walked downstairs into my father's "office," found a stamp and an envelope, and placed the letter in our mailbox.

The next morning when I got up, I found a peanut-butter-and-jelly sandwich in the fridge with a note attached from my mother saying, "You are not a dog." My father, of course, was the only one up, and was sitting in the kitchen reading the paper. Without looking up, he said, "Don't forget to tell everyone the truth today."

I wanted to scream at him and explain the magnitude of the situation. I wanted to tell him that there was a better chance of me shaving my head and walking to school with a dog collar and a leash around my neck than there was of me admitting I had lied.

I walked out the door and it was a beautiful spring day. I had a feeling of hopefulness and excitement that I hadn't had all year. For the first time, I was excited to go to school instead of dreading it the whole way there.

With that wave of confidence came the feeling that I was, in a way, impenetrable. I was the same exact person I had been the day before, but now I was being treated better and the older kids wanted to be friends with me. It didn't matter if I was in a movie or not, I had made these people laugh when they asked me questions. I had found myself engaging, charismatic—even sublime at times. I had all the charm I believed a true movie star to have. Who cares if I had lied about starring in *Private Benjamin Returns*? In the midst of all the commotion, I truly believed something magical had happened. I had burst into womanhood, and never felt more alive. I decided right there and then that I was going to tell the truth.

As I descended the hill where we lived, I spotted Jason at the bottom, standing on the sidewalk in front of his house. There was a part of me that felt bad for him for allowing himself to fall in love with me so quickly, and another part of me that was annoyed that he had so little self-respect. Hadn't he ever seen a Woody Allen movie and realized how to play it cool?

I decided I was going to have to break the news to him first. "Hey," I said, as I reached his house. I knew he'd be disappointed, and I wanted to let him down easy. I didn't want people to ever look back at Chelsea Joy Handler and say she was a fibber.

"Did you hear anything about the movie?" he asked.

"Well, Jason, I have some bad news," I told him. "Goldie broke her collarbone in a hang-gliding accident. It looks like it's been postponed till summer."

"Wow! What a bummer," he said.

"Yeah, but the great news is, I'm in talks to be in one of Madonna's new videos."

"No way!"

"Yup," I told him. "Which means I'm going to have to be on a grueling workout regimen." I had very little control of the things that were flying out of my mouth. All I knew was that it felt better than confessing. Plus, the idea of getting imaginary rock-hard abs was intoxicating.

I knew then that Jason and I could never really build a solid partnership, mostly because our relationship had been based on inconsistencies.

I spent the rest of the week confirming one ridiculous tale after another, and by Friday I was exhausted. Although the benefits of my newfound fame outweighed the burden of coming up with one celebrity tale after another, I was so disgusted and bored with myself after a week, I was ready to throw myself out of my second-story window. I spent upward of an hour contemplating whether or not the fall would actually end my life or just severely injure an ankle. Then I thought of maybe jumping out of one of my father's cars while in motion. This seemed the better option of the two, because not only would I be putting myself out of my misery, I'd also be making a political statement.

I knew if I ever came clean I would look like a complete jackass, so Jodi and I made a pact. She would confirm all my lies, and then after Christmas break the following week, we would slowly plant seeds that I was leaving the business. "I've had enough!" was the phrase we agreed I would use.

The teasing from the older girls had come to a screeching halt, and now when I walked down the halls, almost everyone said hello, and a couple of kids even curtsied. Surprisingly, Principal Hiller never called my house again. Jodi's estimation was that he probably thought he had a psychopath on his hands and felt it was safer to take himself out of the equation.

The Friday afternoon before I was to return to school after Christmas break, Jodi and I were in my sister Sloane's room trying on her training bras when my father yelled my name.

I ran downstairs wearing my sister's bra and a pair of parachute pants when my father handed me a manila envelope without looking up. "You got something in the mail."

I opened the envelope and nearly climaxed. I ran right up to Sloane's room and jumped up and down. "Jodi! Jodi! Look at what I got!" It was a signed autograph from Goldie Hawn. She hadn't inscribed it the way I had requested, and obviously I would hold that against her in any future negotiations, but it was made out to me, and it was signed by her.

Jodi and I were jumping up and down like a pair of newlyweds. We ran into my room and grabbed a Sharpie. Luckily Goldie's handwriting wasn't very legible, so I added "Mom" in parentheses at the end, and, after much discussion, since I didn't want to continue with the lying but wasn't willing to tell the truth either, Jodi and I agreed to leave the note open-ended. This is what I added: "My collarbone is on the mend. Can't wait to start working with you, if the movie ever gets made. Aaargh! You're a star!"

"Well," she said, "it would sure take a lot of guts to come forward now."

"You're absolutely right," I told her, putting the signed photo in my backpack. "Don't let me forget to make copies of this to pass out at school."

After the picture had made its way through school, things started to die down, and only once in awhile would someone mention my movie-star status. In those instances, I made sure not to overembellish the fantasies that played out in my head. I would downplay my role as a Hollywood starlet by telling people I was becoming more and more interested in behind-the-scenes work, and what I really had my eye on was directing.

The lesson I learned that year was a valuable one. If you're going to make up an enormous untruth, make sure you tell it to people you are not spending the rest of the school year with. I can only imagine what Clay Aiken has to deal with on a daily basis.

CHAPTER TWO
Chelsea in Charge

I was twelve years old when I got my boobs. I was over the moon, knowing they were the last piece of the puzzle I needed to start my own business. After sitting my parents down a year earlier and demanding to know the exact status of their financial situation, it had become clear to me that in order for me to have the lifestyle and fulfilling travel experiences that I desired, I would have no choice but to branch out on my own.

"Listen," I said to my mother and father as I began my inquisition, "how much money do you have saved for my bat mitzvah, if, in fact, I do decide to go through with it? Is there any money for sleepaway camp and/or a European teen tour? And last but not least, *do* I have a dowry?" My parents were sitting on the sofa in our summer house in Martha's Vineyard, staring back at me for a good couple of minutes before responding. My father took off his glasses and continued to stare as I stood in front of them holding the deeds to both of our houses.

The fact that we owned a summer house in Martha's Vineyard led most people to believe that we were wealthy when that wasn't the case at all. In the single most savvy business move of my father's lifetime, he purchased ten acres on the Vineyard in the early seventies for a mere $28,000. While Vineyard real-estate prices had since skyrocketed, my father's finances headed in precisely the opposite direction. Even though he owned a valuable piece of real estate, his liquid assets were on par with those of a homeless person—with no hands.

So, even with a decent house in the suburbs and a vacation house on Martha's Vineyard, we had no money. My five older siblings had all decided that college was a necessary evil, leaving my father with even less money for me. I would lie awake night after night, praying that none of them would enter into a serious enough relationship that could lead to an expensive wedding, resulting in a zero balance in my father's savings account—if he even had a savings account.

The afternoon I heard my older brother Greg mention the words "graduate school," I nearly flipped my bicycle. My oldest sister, Sidney, kept reminding me to work hard in school so that I could get a scholarship to my college of choice. This may have been sound advice for an average adolescent, but college directly conflicted with my future plans of becoming a housewife.

"A dowry?" my father asked, as he looked over at my mother. "No, you don't have a dowry."

"Well, what exactly is the plan?" I asked them.

"What plan are you referring to?" my father asked.

"We are going to need to sell one of the houses," I told them. "In my estimation, we could get over a million dollars for this house. I've already contacted a realtor."

"Why would we sell the house, Chelsea?" my mother asked.

"Because things are just not working out," I told them. "First of all, this house is a money pit, and we're not getting any return on our investment. Second, I would like to go to Europe in the fall, not to mention Aruba, Jamaica, and the Bahamas. Third, if I am going to have a bat mitzvah, you can be sure as shit the party's not going to be at a Ramada Inn! And finally, we really need to discuss my wardrobe."

"You're a real piece of work, you know that?" my father said as he got up and walked out of the room.

"Chelsea, please don't use that kind of language," my mother said, referring to my use of the *s* word. "It's very unbecoming. You have to focus on the important things in life, and one day you will realize that it's not all about money."

I had always been suspicious, but from that moment on, I knew without a doubt that my parents and I were not on the same page. We weren't even in the same book. They had no idea how humiliating it was for me, living in a half-Jewish/half-Italian neighborhood where everyone else's families planned big, expensive bar and bat mitzvahs at places like the Four Seasons, the Hyatt Regency, and The Manor. When I asked my parents where we could have mine, "backyard" was the last word I heard before I covered my ears and started making Indian noises. They also had no idea what it was like to watch all my friends prance around in their new designer clothes while I was left wearing hand-me-down Lee jeans from my sister Sloane, who was five years older and twice my size. "Relaxed fit" was an understatement.

My boobs came one May, and luckily for me—and all the men who've felt me up since then—they were full C-cups. I knew then that it was time to start thinking about how they could help me make ends meet. I would be spending the summer on Martha's Vineyard with my parents and my sisters. My brothers were out of college at this point and had real jobs, so they weren't able to take the entire summer off anymore. My father would commute back and forth from New Jersey to the Vineyard for his "business." No one was ever really sure what "business" he was referring to, since he generated roughly the same income as a giraffe.

I was too young to work legally so I only had two realistic options: I could either start my own underground babysitting ring or become a prostitute.

Although I had developed a serious crush on our plumber that year, I wasn't sure that I was ready for penetration. I had seen my very first penis on a porno tape I stole from my brother, and was completely flabbergasted. While I had heard a lot about the size and shape of the penis, no one had ever mentioned that there were going to be balls attached to it. Not to mention that there would be two of them, that they would be covered in hair, and that later in life, they would most likely end up smacking you in the face. I'm really glad I got the heads-up when I did, (a) because if I had found myself in bed with someone and seen his two little friends headed toward me with no prior warning, I probably would have lodged a formal complaint with Internal Affairs, and (b) because it gave me plenty of time to shop for the perfect-size chin guard.

After I took a good long look in the mirror at the two new accessories attached to my upper torso, I decided I could pass for twenty. Sloane said that I was being absurd and that the oldest I could pass for was fifteen. I stood cupping my new breasts, thinking it would probably be best to keep these robust treasures under wraps while I got to know them. So I opted for the babysitting ring and decided I would be sixteen.

Once the decision had been made, I took out the phone book and called every hotel and home rental agency on the island. I left my phone number and told them to direct any guests who needed childcare services my way. The next hurdle was a place to hide all the income I'd be bringing in. I hopped on my ten speed and rode to the hardware store, where I bought myself a safe.

"No one is going to call you back," Sloane told me. "It's a stupid idea and you're not going to make any money. You're certainly not going to need a safe."

"Sloane," I told her, "you either grab life by the balls or you can ride in the back of one of Dad's cars for the rest of your life. With an attitude like that, you're going to end up becoming the general manager of a bowling alley."

Within the first week I received ten calls. By the end of my second week on the Vineyard, every night was booked for the next two weeks. I couldn't believe what a genius I was. Every day and night was packed with a different client, and business was booming. This was a dream come true, and before long Sloane was begging to get in on the action. I would give her clients only if I was overbooked, and insisted she pay me a two-dollar commission per hour. She resisted, of course, but I maintained a level of professionalism through and through. I simply couldn't cut her a break just because she was my sister. "What would my other employees think?" I asked Sloane.

"You don't have any other employees," she reminded me.

"Not the point," I told her.

By mid-July, I had seven hundred dollars saved. Word was spreading like a forest fire, and I actually enjoyed the work. I had a couple of regular clients who were on the island all summer, but most of my clients were only in town for a couple of days or up to a week. Most of the kids were pretty good, and if they weren't, I would just put them to bed as soon as their parents left. I preferred babies since they couldn't talk and tell their parents that I'd spent half the night on the phone talking to my best friend, Jodi, in New Jersey, and the other half of the night going through their personal items.

If the children were annoying, I would play hide-and-seek with them. They would hide, and I would make myself a sandwich or an ice-cream sundae.

If the parents had unreasonable expectations, I'd have a sit-down with them and give it to them straight. "Listen, Melinda," I told a mother who insisted I take her six-month-old daughter to swimming classes twice a week. "Are you trying to kill your baby? She can't do that yet. She's not a salmon."

One day I got a phone call from a woman named Susan who was renting a house in town. She had two sons.

"My oldest is fourteen and my youngest is seventy-two months," she informed me.

While I sat perplexed trying to figure out what seventy-two months added up to, I decided to focus on the bigger issue at hand.

"Fourteen?" I asked. Who hires a babysitter for a fourteen-year-old? I wondered if he was retarded. "Is he retarded?" I asked.

"No, he's not retarded," the woman replied, sounding a little shocked. "He's just a little hyper, but he's a good boy. It's more to have someone else there who can be in charge of my youngest, Kyle."

"Uh-huh," I said, as I took a bite out of the apple I was holding and kicked my feet up on the sofa. "Well, I charge ten dollars an hour for two kids."

She said that sounded reasonable, and we set a time for the next evening.

"Who was that?" Sloane asked as I hung up the phone.

"A client," I told her. "I have to babysit for a fourteen-year-old tomorrow."

"You can't babysit for a fourteen-year-old," Sloane told me.

"Why not?"

"Because you're twelve, that's why!"

"They don't know how old I am," I said, as I polished off my apple and penciled my new client into my Filofax.

"Chelsea, you can't babysit for someone who is two years older than you," Sloane said.

"Girls mature faster than boys," I reminded her. "It'll be fine."

The next night my father dropped me off at Susan's house. He was impressed with my work ethic and business sense. "You've really shown a strong sense of self, Chels. I'm proud of you," my father told me.

"Thanks, Dad," I said as I hopped out of the car. "If you need to borrow any cash, I'm sure we can work something out at a moderate interest rate."

I walked up the steps and peered through the screen door. "Hello," I said. Susan came running to the door, carrying her seventy-two-month-old son on her hip.

"Oh, Chelsea, it's so lovely to meet you." She was harried and it didn't take long to figure out that she was completely unstable. "This is Kyle," she said in baby talk as she introduced me to the kid she was holding like a baby kangaroo. "Can you say hello to Chelsea?" she asked him as she took the pacifier out of his six-year-old mouth.

"Hi," he said shyly, and then nuzzled his head into Susan's shoulder.

"Let's go in and meet James."

James was her fourteen-year-old and I half expected him to be in a crib, but instead he was sitting on the living room floor playing Nintendo. I sized him up and figured we were about the same size, although it looked like he had a bit more lean muscle mass than I did, which would give him the advantage if it came down to a tug-of-war.

"He loves those video games," she said, shaking her head.

"Kids," I said, shaking my head in unison. I wanted Susan to think we were totally in sync, even though it was becoming very obvious that Susan needed to be under psychiatric supervision. I followed her to the kitchen, where she had three pages of telephone numbers listed in case of an emergency. At the very top of the list in bold print was: ANY SORT OF EMERGENCY: DIAL 911.

Then it went on to list every family member still alive, including a few relatives she had in Russia. I tried to picture myself calling overseas to Moscow if and when Kyle hanged himself. I couldn't believe someone like Susan would allow a complete stranger to babysit her children.

"I know this is a bit extensive but I just wanted to cover all bases."

"Hello, I'm James Sr.," her husband said meekly as he walked into the kitchen. He looked like a battered wife with his head hung low and his terrible posture. I immediately felt sorry for him.

Susan and I spent the next forty-five minutes going over the boys' routines. "Their pajamas are already laid out. Kyle goes down at seven thirty and James can stay up till nine o'clock and watch a show. Both can have some frozen yogurt after dinner but only the sugar-free kind. There is a tub of vanilla-chocolate swirl ice cream in the freezer for James Sr. The children are not allowed to have that." Then she leaned in and whispered, "James Jr. is a sugar addict."

"Does he go to meetings?" I asked her.

"He can be very moody. We try and stabilize his blood sugar level, and if he's on his best behavior, he can have one or two spoonfuls of regular ice cream, but anything more than that and he tends to get carried away."

I wanted to tell Susan that the reason James Jr. probably got carried away was because he was living in the equivalent of a state penitentiary, and that she was doing far more damage than good to these children by treating them like they were both infants.

After weeks of childcare over the summer, it became obvious that the best contribution I could make to the world would be to open up my very own day-care/night-care center. Clearly I knew more about child-rearing than most of the parents I had encountered. Sugar addict? Who isn't a sugar addict when they're fourteen? I, of course, couldn't speak for myself at the time, being only twelve.

Susan was the antithesis of my mother. There was more adult supervision at the Neverland Ranch than there was in my house growing up. When a week before my fourth birthday, my parents told me to plan my own birthday party—I knew I was pretty much on my own.

My brothers and sisters occasionally stepped in with some guidance, but my parents were exhausted after raising my five older siblings, and I have no doubt that my mother's pregnancy with me was an accident. Mostly because on several occasions, she told me I was an accident.

I wanted Susan and her husband to leave already, and wondered if she would ever stop talking. I had dealt with some over-protective parents before, but this was outrageous.

Susan was a total basket case, and I didn't like the idea of being responsible for either one of her children. This was clearly a woman who would fly off the handle if she came home to find one of her kids missing.

The whole time Susan was talking, James Sr. sat at the kitchen table staring out the window. He probably had no idea his life would end up like this when he first met Susan. She was probably fun and outgoing with no signs of being a complete and utter nightmare. This was not the life anyone intended to carve out for themselves, and I imagined James Sr. hanging himself sometime in the next couple of weeks.

After explaining in excruciatingly painful detail what to do in case of a tidal wave, she handed Kyle to me and headed for the door. When they finally left, I put Kyle down on his feet, and we walked back into the living room, where James Jr. was playing Nintendo.

"I want my dinner," James said, without looking up from the game he was playing.

"Okay," I said, and walked back in the kitchen with Kyle, who was shadowing my every move.

"Actually," he yelled out, "I'll take some frozen yogurt first."

I didn't mind giving James the frozen yogurt first, but didn't really appreciate being ordered around like a servant. "Well, would you like to come into the kitchen and eat it?"

"No, bring it to me!" he barked.

I looked down at Kyle, who frowned and shrugged his

shoulders. "Do you want frozen yogurt first too?" I asked him. Kyle's eyes lit up as he nodded his head feverishly. Kyle was cute and I felt bad for him. He had no chance of having a normal life. If I had just been a couple of years older, I could have adopted Kyle and given him a real life, but I knew I had to get through middle school before committing myself to potty training a six-year-old.

"I'll get the yogurt for you," Kyle said in a very soft, sweet voice. I was shocked that in his condition he could even speak, never mind negotiate his way to the freezer.

"Thank you, Kyle, that's very thoughtful of you," I said loudly, eyeing James to let him know that good behavior would be rewarded with positive affirmations. "What a sweet boy you are!"

I kept a close watch on James until Kyle returned with the bowl and walked over to where his brother was sitting.

"Put it on the floor," James demanded.

"Can you please not talk to him like that?" I asked James in what I thought was a reasonable tone.

What happened next is hard to describe. Whatever happened to Lou Ferrigno right before he turned into the Incredible Hulk was similar to the rage that filled up James's face right before he wailed, "Put the yogurt on the floor!" The only differences were, James didn't turn green and he wasn't wearing cut-off jeans. Kyle started crying and I nearly threw my back out picking him up.

I felt a little scared but was also taken aback by the lack of respect James had for adults. He was obviously a loose cannon, and I knew I had to remain calm and get back some control of the situation.

"Okay, James, you need to pipe down. I do not appreciate being talked to like that, and you are scaring your brother."

"I don't have to listen to you. I can talk to you any way I want, you dumb girl!"

I was tempted to tell James that he was technically talking to a woman, since my very first period had come on a like a sneak attack earlier that month, but I wasn't about to get into the birds and bees discussion so early in the night.

This was not going well, and I really had no idea what to do. I was trying to console Kyle while racking my brain trying to think of the best approach for handling an unruly teenager.

"That's it," I told him. "You're getting a time-out." I walked over to the television and shut it off. This sent James into a full-blown meltdown. He threw his game control at the window but stayed seated while he pounded his fists into the floor over and over again and started bawling. I hadn't been alone with them for five minutes, and now both kids were crying and one of them was foaming at the mouth. I made a mental note to ask for more money when their parents returned.

"Okay, calm down, James, just calm down. Please stop crying." I put Kyle down because my knees were giving out. "Please, everyone stop crying." I went and turned the TV back on. James immediately perked up and went to retrieve his game control.

"Not so fast," I told him. "You are fourteen years old and you have no business acting like this."

"Shut up, stupid," he grunted, as he craned his neck around where I was standing to get a look at the TV screen. I couldn't believe what an asshole this kid was. I was obviously going to have to give him a spanking.

"Listen up, James," I told him, standing my ground. "I am not trying to make your life miserable; it obviously already is. But there is no need to take your frustration out on me." Kyle was now standing next to me, holding on to my pant leg and sniffling, his pacifier in his mouth. "Now say you're sorry," I said to James.

"No!" he screamed. "No fucking way!"

I wanted to hit James. I thought about a closed-fist punch and then my mind drifted to a swift kick in the neck. "That's it," I said, shutting off the television once more. "You are going to bed, mister."

"The fuck I am!" he screamed as he got to his feet. He was taller than I had originally estimated and towered over me. This was getting scary and I knew my personal safety was in danger. No matter what, the first rule of babysitting was never to show any fear.

"I'm calling your parents," I told James as I held Kyle's hand and walked out of the living room into the kitchen, where I spotted a huge tub of vanilla-chocolate swirl ice cream on the counter.

"Kyle, that's not frozen yogurt, that's ice cream."

Kyle, who clearly wouldn't know the difference between

a guitar and an airplane, shrugged his shoulders and started to cry.

"It's okay, Kyle. It's okay," I assured him, kneeling down to give him a hug.

"I'll be good," Hitler Jr. called after me in a completely calm tone of voice.

I turned around and walked back into the living room, where he had stopped crying and was seated on the floor next to his half-eaten bowl of ice cream. "You were not supposed to have sugar, James."

"It's what Kyle gave me," he said, shrugging his shoulders innocently. "I'm not a sugar addict, it's fine. My mom is nuts."

"Well, that's obvious," I told him, finally feeling like we had made a connection. "But I'm supposed to be watching you, and she told me not to let you have any, so do me a favor and don't tell her, and I won't either."

"Cool," he said, actually looking in my direction for the first time since I had arrived.

Kyle was finally calming down, and if he hadn't put his arms up for me to pick him up again, I would have given myself an actual pat on the back for finding a way to reason with James. *I really am good with kids*, I thought to myself.

"I'm going to my room," James announced as he got up abruptly and marched out of the living room—and then came back in. "And don't come up there, you dirty bitch!"

I didn't know what to make of James. I didn't know if he suffered from Tourette's or bipolar disorder. I did not feel safe at all, and it occurred to me that I would need to start carrying a taser gun.

I looked down at Kyle, who had taken his pacifier out of his mouth and was eating James's leftover ice cream, and I wondered if he was still breast-feeding.

After Kyle was done I told him it was bedtime. It was only 7 p.m., but I needed some time alone to prepare myself in case Hannibal Lecter came back downstairs. I changed Kyle's diaper, helped him into his pajamas, read him *Goodnight Moon*, and then tucked him in. "Good luck with everything," I told him before I turned out his light.

I walked over to James's room and knocked on the door. I thought about what it must be like for James to go through life under these conditions, with a mother like Susan. It's no wonder he was miserable. I thought maybe I could sit down and talk to him about his life, be a shoulder he could cry on, if for no other reason than to prevent him from becoming a date-raper later in life. "Do you want me to bring you your dinner?" I asked through the closed door. Silence.

I was about to ask again, but decided I was the one who needed to eat dinner. All this caretaking had made me forget about my own needs. I went downstairs and looked in the fridge. There were a few containers that had JAMES SR. written on them. I took one out, opened it, and found some chicken. After taking a couple of bites and not being able to identify the exact spice used in preparing it, I shut the container and put it back in the fridge. I went over to the cupboard and found a can of SpaghettiOs.

About an hour later the phone rang right in the middle of a brand-new episode of *The Golden Girls*. My favorite character was Bea Arthur. I've always felt we had similar senses of humor, although I imagined myself having a much better body when I hit seventy, not to mention highlights.

I picked up the phone and Susan was on the other end. "Hi, Chelsea, is everything okay?"

"Yes, everything is fine," I told her, feeling like I had finally gotten the situation under control, and not wanting to miss any more of *The Golden Girls* than necessary.

"That's wonderful, Chelsea. Thank you so much."

"No problem, Suz," I told her. "Have fun at the movie."

The minute I hung up the phone James walked into the room with the entire bucket of frozen yogurt along with the entire bucket of vanilla-chocolate swirl ice cream in his hands. Both were empty. I hadn't had any experience with sugar mania before, but was intuitive enough to know things were not going well.

He ran in and started jumping up and down on the couch I was sitting on. This was way before Tom Cruise humiliated himself on *Oprah*, and I had no idea then that James's behavior was not only a result of liking sugar, but most likely a direct link to Scientology.

"No more monkeys jumping on the bed!" he started screaming.

I was so shocked at first, I pretended he wasn't doing anything out of the ordinary and tried to ignore him. If he was looking for attention, he wasn't going to get it from me. Then he jumped off the couch, ran into the kitchen, and came back with two oranges, both which he fired in my direction. One hit me right in the forehead, and the other went through the window, breaking the glass.

Once I got hit in the face, I lost my cool. I stood up, but before I could make my move, James pushed me back down onto the couch. Not only was I petrified of what might happen next, I was furious that I would mostly likely have a bruise in the middle of my forehead, with Ash Wednesday months away.

I had to think quickly. I decided the best approach was to not react at all, so I sat there watching him buzz around the room, banging his head into one wall after another. I remained seated, not wanting to run any interference and get manhandled. I knew James would crash, but I didn't know how long that was going to take, and was praying he would get it under control by the end of the commercial break. The last five minutes of *The Golden Girls* were right around the corner, and the episode's plot line was clearly leading up to a cliffhanger.

James was a real live windup toy and I was just hoping his batteries would die soon. I looked at the broken window and wondered what I was going to tell his parents. I didn't even care. I just wanted to go home. I thought about my sister Sloane and how she would have handled this situation . . . Sloane would never have *been* in this situation, because she was about as much fun as a cold sore, and would have never allowed anyone to eat an entire tub each of ice cream and frozen yogurt, even if it wasn't intentional.

Then James picked up one of the tubs, tossed it on the floor, and eyed me like a piece of meat. I pretended I didn't notice his death stare, and even tried to fake a yawn as an example of my disinterest in his showcase.

I was successful in faking disinterest until he took the almost-empty ice cream tub and forced it over my head. "Stop it!" I screamed, kicking my legs while my head was getting coated in vanilla-chocolate swirl. He was spinning the tub around my head and I was getting ice cream leftovers in my mouth, eyes, and nose. I felt myself starting to hyperventilate. I couldn't take another minute, and tried to head-butt my way out the other end of the carton, but without enough wiggle room found it nearly impossible. I had no choice but to find my way between James's legs and nail him in the balls with my foot.

As James went flying onto the ground, I took off my ice-cream hat, threw it on the floor, and got on top of him like a wrestler, pinning his biceps down with my knees. "Listen, you little fucker, I am going to call the police on your ass, you crazy lunatic bitch! What the hell is the matter with you?"

Tears were streaming down his face. It was a sad moment; even though he had attacked me like an ice-cream ninja, I couldn't help but feel awful for him.

"I'm sorry I kicked you in your privates," I told him, awkwardly maintaining my position on top of him. (A position, mind you, that I became much more comfortable with later on in life.) "But you are a mess. What is wrong with you?"

"I'm sorry," he said softly.

I finally felt like maybe the sugar was passing through his

body, and I could tell he was tired from crying. I knew that whenever I threw a temper tantrum, I always felt pretty beat afterward as well. I got up from sitting on his penis.

"I'm going to bed," he said, and walked upstairs to his bedroom.

I sat on the sofa, staring at the empty container of yogurt, wondering how long I was going to have this headache. James Sr. and Susan walked in moments after I had finished cleaning up.

"How were they?" Susan asked as she walked into the living room.

"Fine, they were fine," I said, standing in front of the broken window.

"There were no problems?"

"Nope," I told her.

"Really?"

"Yes, they were perfect."

I thought about the benefits of telling her the truth about what had happened, but knew that with all the details, I could have spent another four hours in that house, and, truth be told, I wanted to go home and wash my hair.

James Sr. grabbed my jacket and we both headed outside to the car. He was very sweet and told me how nice it was to have dinner without any kids. He seemed like a submissive type of guy who was being tortured on a daily basis by his family. His life was not his own, and I knew he would be the perfect prototype for my first husband. As we headed down the dirt road leading to my parents' house, he said, "I really can't tell you how grateful I am for you babysitting," he said. "We never really get a chance to go out."

"No problem," I told him. "My pleasure."

"By the way," I added. "James Junior threw an orange through the living room window and it's broken, and then he took an empty tub of ice cream and crowned me with it until I had to wrestle him to the floor." I left out the kicking-him-in-the-nuts part, because I didn't want any of the blame in this scenario.

James Sr. didn't respond to what I said immediately, and when he did, he said, "I had a feeling things got hairy when I saw the back of your hair matted to your head. I suppose you would never want to babysit for us again, huh?" It was clear to me that James Sr. needed to leave his wife, but was one of those men who would never have the guts. Instead, he would rather suffer 90 percent of the time in anticipation of the small capsules of grown-up time he could have with her. And even though that had been one of the worst nights of my life, I wasn't going to be the one responsible for denying him his only morsel of happiness.

"I have a sister named Sloane who is older than me and has much more experience with emotional illness. I think you'll like her. And I think she'll really get a kick out of James Junior. The only problem is that she charges $15 an hour."

"That'll be fine," James Sr. told me.

"And she carries Mace," I added.

CHAPTER THREE

Prison Break

It was exactly one week after my twenty-first birthday when I got my first DUI. I haven't gotten another one since, but I'm not ruling anything out.

My friend Lydia and I were on our way home from a night of heavy drinking and were midway through the second chorus of Whitney Houston's "I Wanna Dance with Somebody" when she punched me in the shoulder and slurred, "I think you're getting pulled over."

"Huh?" I asked as I hurriedly readjusted my rearview mirror, which I had been using in place of a compact. I lowered the volume on the radio and turned my head around for confirmation of what looked eerily similar to glaring red lights. Lydia was right. I was getting pulled over. "Fuck."

I've always had a fear of police officers, especially when their sirens are blaring and they're behind me. "Don't say anything," I ordered as I quickly slammed on the brakes and drove over the curb and into a stop sign.

Lydia slurs when she's sober, never mind after seven vodkas with cranberry juice. She also has a tendency to offend people who can help us. Earlier that evening we had gone to a seventies revival bar in Westwood where the bouncer wouldn't let us in unless we were on the list. "I'll handle this," she said, right before she laid into him. "What, do you think you're special because you're a bouncer? Puh-lease. You're not an authority figure. You know you're just fat and stupid, right? Now, can we come in or what?"

"Pretend you're sleeping," I barked at her as I saw two police officers get out of the patrol car.

"You weren't doing anything. Tell them you want proof!"

"I'm serious, Lydia, shut up. Do not say a word, and close your eyes! Go to sleep."

A burly officer in his late thirties approached my side of the car while his partner tapped a flashlight on Lydia's window, motioning for her to roll it down as he shined the flashlight in her face.

Lydia had to open the door because the window didn't roll down. For my twenty-first birthday a week earlier, my father had shipped me a 1985 two-door Yugo with one working window. The year was 1996 and, as luck would have it, the window that worked was on the driver side, in the backseat. Forgetting my window didn't roll down, I had tried on several occasions to throw a cigarette out of it, only to repeatedly slam my left hand into the glass. I had started physical therapy a few weeks prior in order to get some of the strength back in my hand, but was having trouble making a full recovery because, as the therapist said, my injury was "highly unusual."

"Hi, sir," I said to the policeman as I opened my door. "Sorry, my windows don't roll down." I was trying to keep one eye on my cop and one eye on Lydia, knowing that any chance I had of getting out of this situation was going to depend entirely on my performance.

"License and registration" was his hello to me.

"Sure," I slurred as I stood up, leaning one hand on my door. As I rifled through my purse for my license, I said to him as articulately as I could, "Can you ask me why I pulled you over?"

The officer smirked at his partner, who was asking Lydia to remain seated in the car, and then looked back at me. "I'm going to need you to step away from your vehicle, ma'am."

"Ma'am?" I asked, trying to figure out how old I actually was since I had been lying about my age for some time in order to get into bars. I couldn't remember if I was legally or illegally drunk.

"Where are you coming from, Miss . . . Handler?"

"Baja Fresh!" Lydia yelled from inside the car.

My officer stared at me while I tried to think of anything that rhymed with Baja Fresh that would also be open at two o'clock in the morning.

"Her cat died," I told my cop. "She's really tired."

"Uh-huh, it says on your license . . ."

"Oh, shit," I said, and grabbed the license I had given

him to make sure it was mine and not the fake one that said I was my twenty-six-year-old Mormon sister, Sloane. It was my license. I handed it back to him. "Sorry."

"It says here that you live up the street," he continued as he pointed in the direction behind us. I realized then that I had driven past my own apartment.

"Tell him you want to make your phone call!" Lydia screamed.

"You haven't even asked me if I've been drinking." I paused. Then I leaned in with my index finger pointed at him. "Because I haven't been . . . if that's what you're getting at."

"Really?" he asked.

"Nope, don't like the taste," I said matter-of-factly. "I had two drinks, that's all. . . . Okay, three drinks."

"Tell him about your cold," Lydia crowed once more from the car, which was now twenty feet away from where we were standing.

"She has a cold," I said, and then started again. "I mean, we both have colds. We've both taken a significant amount of Robitussin, so if there's anything on my breath, that's what you're smelling. I caught my cold from a homeless person at one of the shelters downtown where I was volunteering."

"Please stay in the car, ma'am," I heard the other officer say to Lydia as she once again tried to get out.

"Go to sleep!" I yelled back at her.

"Okay, Miss Handler, I'm going to need you to stand with your legs apart, your hands out, and your eyes closed." This sounded exactly as I had imagined my first DUI to sound:

very authoritative and just like in the movies. I got into position and knew there was no chance I'd be arrested. I had practiced this procedure many times with Lydia late at night in our apartment.

"Let me guess what's next." I giggled. "Touch my nose with my index finger, I suppose."

"That's exactly right," he said. "Have you done this before?"

"Yeah," I told him. "Plenty of times."

Had they not come up with any new sobriety test moves in recent years? I actually felt bad for him for a minute. It was a shame that the police weren't smarter. I did what was asked of me and then he told me to walk in a straight line with one foot in front of the other.

"My heels are too high," I told him. "I wouldn't be able to do that sober."

"Well, you can either take them off or take a Breathalyzer."

"You're turning into a real nightmare," I said as I leaned one hand on his large shoulder and took my heels off. "Okay, you know what? I had one drink. One very small drink."

This is when Lydia decided to slide over to the driver's side of the car and climb out. "Ma'am, I told you to stay in the car, and if you don't listen, I'm going to have to handcuff you and read you your rights," her officer said.

"Lydia, stop it!" I yelled. "Sit down!"

"Faggot!" was her next attempt at mollifying the situation.

"All right, miss," said her officer as he whipped out his handcuffs. "You've been warned, and now I'm placing you under arrest and taking you to jail." Upon hearing that, I immediately fell over and hit the pavement with one heel on and one heel off.

I looked up at my officer, knowing this was not going the way I had planned. "She always gets like this when she has a cold, plus with her dog dying and everything, please don't arrest—"

He interrupted me as he helped me to my feet. "I thought it was her cat."

"It's a hybrid," I mumbled as I looked down at my freshly pedicured toes, wondering why they couldn't all just be the same length.

"Miss, you can either take a Breathalyzer here, or we can test your urine down at the station. Which would you prefer?"

"That depends," I said. "Is there any way to detect marijuana through a Breathalyzer?"

Lydia was now sobbing heavily while also screaming obscenities at her cop as she was being escorted into their squad car.

"Let's go," he said. "We'll take you downtown for a urine test."

"No," I said. "I don't even have to go to the bathroom."

"Fine," he said, and went to retrieve the invention I now feel immense hatred for—the Breathalyzer is second only to the answering machine, which has led to three separate breakups.

It turned out that I was, in fact, intoxicated. I blew a 2.4, which far exceeds the legal limit of 0.8.

Once handcuffed in the squad car next to Lydia, my blood really began to boil. "So this is how it's gonna go down, huh?

You can't just turn around, drive the fifty yards back to my house, and drop us off? NO! Of course not, because I fought the law and the law won!"

After a pause I murmured "racist" under my breath, loud enough for both of them to hear.

The cop in the passenger seat turned around with a confused look on his face. "We're all white."

"Whatever," I said.

"Well . . . still" was Lydia's comeback.

"I'm Jewish," I told them. No response. "Did you hear me?" I said. "This is racial profiling, and I won't be a party to it. Let me out!"

"Anti-Samoans!" Lydia yelled.

"You girls will be released when you sober up. You'll be charged with a DUI, Miss Handler, and your friend will be charged with being drunk and disorderly. Would you like us to add obstruction of justice to those charges, or would you two like to be quiet until we get down to the station?"

"There better be air-conditioning there," I mumbled.

"We're going to prison!" Lydia bawled. She was still sobbing heavily.

"Don't worry. Just calm down. My father's an attorney."

"No, he's not," Lydia replied.

"Shut up," I growled. "What's going to happen to my car?" I asked the officers.

"It will be impounded," the officer said.

"More great news," I huffed. "Is this going to be an overnight thing?"

"We'll release you girls when you sober up," replied the cop who was driving.

"Well, then, can we at least stop by my apartment so I can get my contact solution?" I asked him.

Once again both officers ignored me, and Lydia was now moaning like she had been mauled by a grizzly bear. As ridiculous and belligerent as Lydia was, I still felt bad for her. I have a very hard time maintaining my composure when I see anyone cry. It only takes a few seconds for me to start crying too, which has ruled out any chance of me becoming a rape crisis counselor.

"Okay, girls, let's get you booked," my cop said as we pulled up to the police station. He got out of the car and opened my door. Finally, some chivalry.

We went through the motions of the fingerprints, photo shoot, and paperwork. Then we were thrown into a holding cell with one other woman who looked like Courtney Love's twin sister.

"What about our phone call?" I asked the female officer who brought us two blankets.

"Would you like to make one?" she asked.

I looked at Lydia, who was already sleeping in the fetal position on her blanket.

"Yes . . . no, just forget it!" I yelled, realizing no one we knew would be sober enough to pick us up.

I looked at Courtney Love's doppelgänger biting her nails. She had no shoes on and her feet were filthy. She was wearing a white pleather miniskirt and sitting with her legs wide open.

I smiled at her.

"Fuck off" was her response.

"Roger that," I said, and turned to lie down.

I don't remember falling asleep, but I do remember an officer coming into our cell a couple of hours later when it was light out.

"Okay, Lydia Davis. You can go now. You're being released. Chelsea—who's Chelsea?" I sat up and raised my hand. "Okay, yes, you're going to be transported downtown to Sybil Brand."

"Huh? What's that?"

"That's the Los Angeles County women's prison," Courtney Love chimed in.

"What? Why?"

The female officer looked down at some paperwork in her hand. "We ran your name in our computer and there seems to be an outstanding warrant for your arrest, for fraud. Something about using your sister's identification. Someone reported you to the Federal Bureau of Investigation, and you have been on the government's watch list for a year and a half."

"The government's watch list? Don't you think that's a little dramatic? I was using it to get into bars!" I exclaimed, now in tears. "She gave it to me," I lied, trying to pin the blame on my sister.

"Well, it says here that she was the one who filed the complaint," the officer informed me.

"What?"

I couldn't believe what a nightmare my sister was. My own sister. How could she be so stupid? What was her problem, anyway? It's not like I was using her license to rent apartments or apply for credit cards. All I wanted to do was get a little buzz going.

"There's a bus that comes down here after picking up the inmates in Malibu, and it will take you to Sybil Brand, where they will put you into the system and you'll stay there until someone posts your bail."

"Bail?" I asked. This was turning into a bad episode of *Law & Order*. "How much is my bail?"

"Ten percent of $100,000, which is $10,000," she told me.

"That's not bad," Courtney Love chimed in. "Mine's $15,000."

"Don't worry, Chels, I'll figure it out," Lydia said.

Now *I* was crying, and Lydia hugged me. "I'm not leaving you. I'll go to prison with you."

"You can't stay with me," I sniffled.

"Okay," she said, and walked out.

The policewoman shut the gate to our cell, and Lydia peered through two of the bars. "We'll figure it out, Chels. Do you want me to call your dad?"

"No!" I did kind of want her to call my father because I wanted him to hit my sister, but I definitely didn't want him to know I had gotten a DUI. My aunt and uncle were lushes and lived in Bel-Air with their nine children. They'd be far more understanding.

"Call my aunt," I said to Lydia, as my mind shifted back and forth from how I was going to brush my teeth to whether or not I would have access to the Internet in prison. There was much planning to be done if I truly was going to prison: My first priority was to start thinking about what kind of gang I would join.

I hoped my uncle wasn't still mad at me for choosing to have sex with a family friend instead of him when my cousins and I were playing the "Who Would You Rather Have Sex With?" game. The premise of the game is you have to choose between two people who you would rather have sex with—sober—or your entire family is killed. Usually, the choice is between two real winners like David Hasselhoff and Gary Coleman. A couple of weeks prior, when my fourteen-year-old cousin Madison asked me if I would rather have sex with her dad (my uncle) or their family friend Rusty, I of course chose Rusty, because he was not a *relative*. My uncle didn't take kindly to this when Madison told him. He took it as a personal insult that I would rather have sex with someone I barely knew. "We are related!" I told him.

"That's really shitty, Chelsea," he replied as he took another sip of his double vodka and grapefruit. "I've been like an uncle to you."

"You *are* my uncle," I reminded him.

"Not by blood," he replied.

A couple hours later a female officer came in and handcuffed me. "The bus is here to take you to Sybil Brand."

"I hope you realize that you're making a big mistake," I told her. "My father works for the Department of Sanitation."

"Well, then, you should have no problem getting released."

She smiled. She walked me on the bus and sat me down next to a Hispanic woman with two gold front teeth who looked like she was in her nineties. Then the female officer shackled our ankles together.

"Are you being serious?" I asked her. "Do you really think ankle cuffs are necessary? I am not an outlaw."

"Standard operating procedure," she replied.

I looked around the bus at all the other prisoners. There were close to twenty women altogether. The only race not represented was Asian, and I breathed a sigh of relief. Mandarin and Cantonese are two dialects I knew wouldn't be easy to pick up, not to mention the pressure that would come with joining an Asian gang. This was years before the release of *Crouching Tiger, Hidden Dragon*, and my martial arts weren't anywhere near the level they are today.

I looked over at the woman shackled to my ankle and made the peace sign.

She didn't respond, so I had no choice but to vocalize it. "Peace," I said, leaning in to make sure she could hear me.

"Peace," she responded without looking in my direction.

I turned around to look at the two black women sitting directly behind me. One looked like she'd only be a voice if she lost any more weight, and the other was about four hundred pounds and looked like she was very close to eating the woman sitting next to her.

I lifted my chin and jutted it in their direction. "Word."

A cold stare met my eyes from Fat Albert's sister, and the skinny woman kept staring out the window, shaking. "You wanna get bitch-slapped, Barbie?" was the next thing I heard from a black woman sitting behind Fat Albert's sister.

I was tempted to let Foxy Brown know that it wasn't really possible for anyone to bitch-slap me with handcuffs on, but decided to keep a low profile. I turned around and wondered when Malibu had become so heavily integrated.

The bus ride lasted for about forty-five minutes, and I kept to myself the rest of the trip. It became clear that this wasn't my crowd and that once I got to prison I would have to find the girls with good teeth and run with them.

Once we got to Sybil Brand, all twenty of us were put into a holding cell with benches, while they would call us out one by one to be booked and fingerprinted again. They unshackled us, and the minute Goldfinger was separated from me, she walked over to a corner of the room, pulled her pants down, and peed on the floor.

It was quickly becoming apparent to me that this situation was much more serious than I had realized. This was turning into a full-blown episode of *Survivor: Women of the Outback*. Not only were some of these woman behaving like wild Indians, but looking around the room, I knew that if I had any hopes of blending in here, I would have no choice but to get a tattoo.

Soon after we arrived, an officer came in with a bunch of sandwiches covered in Saran Wrap. You would have thought these women were getting food airlifted in a war zone. One woman was knocked to the ground as others ran to the officer bearing sandwiches.

How anyone could have a sandwich at a time like this was beyond my imagination. I stayed seated on my bench and watched this pandemonium in disgust. I avoided further eye contact with any of the women until finally my name was called.

I was taken in to be booked and fingerprinted. Again, I tried explaining to the officer taking my picture that this was a huge mistake, and that they shouldn't bother booking me, as I was going to be bailed out at any minute.

"That's what they all say, sweetie," she replied.

"I'm serious," I said as I turned my head to the side for my profile shot. "My father is black."

She told me it didn't matter what race my father was, and that even if my bail had already been posted, I couldn't be released until I was entered into the system.

Next up was a strip search, or what I now refer to as anal rape. They took us in groups of eight into another holding area, where we were instructed to undress and stand a few feet away from each other in the buff. This news, of course, threw me into a hissy fit, as I tried to piece together when I had last had a bikini wax. It had been at least a month, and I knew it was not going to be pretty. Even though I am not an extremely unkempt girl, I make it a personal rule to never allow others the displeasure of seeing my beaver in an unruly state.

Turns out that I had nothing to worry about. Once we were all undressed, I realized the true meaning of "unruly." There were women in there who clearly had never heard of a razor, never mind a bikini wax. Hedge trimmers would have been a more appropriate tool for the situations going on in between some of these women's legs. One woman looked like she had Buckwheat stuck in a leglock.

As each woman bent over and spread her ass cheeks, I wondered what the officers thought they would find. "I'm sorry," I blurted out. "I can tell you right now that I do not have anything inside my brown eye. You do not have to check it."

"Ma'am, please turn around and bend over," the female officer said to me.

"I just don't understand what you think you're going to find in there," I said, standing upright with both hands covering my asshole.

"You'd be surprised, ma'am—drugs, pills, money. Yesterday someone had a Game Boy up in there."

"A Game Boy?" I asked, horrified. I turned around and tried to relax my butt cheeks. "Were the batteries in it?"

"Uh-huh," she replied as she motioned for me to get into position.

"I guess that gives new meaning to the term 'junk in your trunk.'" No one responded to my joke, which I thought was extremely clever. I turned around and bent over. It wasn't as unpleasant as I had expected, but I would have been much less inclined to put up a fight if the officer were male.

Afterward we were each given a bright orange two-piece prison suit and open-toed slippers. Fortunately the slippers really showed off my pedicure, but the orange prison garb was a total nightmare for my skin tone. I had found out years earlier that I was a "summer" and the best colors for me were pastels.

I looked at the clock and saw that it was 7:30 p.m. If I wasn't here, I would be leaving happy hour this very minute, most likely with someone of South American descent.

Finally, they led the eight of us into a room the size of a football field filled with rows of bunk beds. There were hundreds of women everywhere, and none of them looked Jewish. I was assigned to a top bunk in the middle of the room. The bottom bunk, I had to assume, was occupied by the large muscular woman doing one-armed push-ups next to it. I was given a bag of toiletries, and when I looked inside and didn't find a pair of eyeshades, I nearly hit the roof.

The situation was growing worse by the minute. I looked at G.I. Jane and asked her if there was a manager around.

"Huh?" she asked.

"Hi, sorry, I'm Chelsea," I said, putting out my hand. When she didn't meet my hand for a handshake, I asked her who was in charge around here.

"Depends. What are you looking for?"

"Well, I'm not supposed to be here, so I need to talk to whoever's in charge."

"Go to the window up front; the guards don't know nothin'."

"Thanks," I said, and walked over to the glass partition at the front of the room, only to be stared at by every woman I passed.

"She looks yummy," I heard someone say as I sped up and stared at the ground. I was in no mood to fight off a sexual abuser. Normally I would never be one to report a rape, unless, of course, it ended badly. But if my attacker was a woman, that opened up an entirely new playing field.

When I got to the booth, there were about fifteen women in line ahead of me waiting to speak with the two women behind the large glass partition. It struck me that this was exactly like the DMV, except we were all wearing the same jumpsuits. There was a large Mexican woman in front of me with a shaved head and tattoos covering both of her arms. She turned around to look at me and didn't drop her stare for thirty seconds. I had already learned through trial and error that the conventional "hello" or "word up" didn't work here, so to break the awkward silence I had to try something new. "I like your head."

She said something in Spanish and spit on my feet. Then she looked at me again for an uncomfortably long time. I gave her a closed-mouth smile to let her know I was totally cool with her spitting on me, until she turned back around. She had two large knots above the roll of fat that connected her head to her shoulders, and her back was the size of a suitcase. This was the type of woman you'd want on your side if you were up against a crocodile.

I looked around at all the inmates milling about. Some were in groups talking, one woman was rapping loudly with headphones on, and there was some sort of frenzy ensuing in the far corner of the room about fifty yards away. Then I heard yelling. "Ham-and-cheese sandwiches!" Again, I saw all the women flocking to one area as sandwiches flew through the air, some landing on beds, some landing in people's outstretched hands. Everyone in line in front of me scattered and ran toward the sandwiches. It was a complete madhouse and gave whole new meaning to the word "picnic."

I, of course, seized this opportunity to get to the front of the line and get some answers. "Hello," I said to the officer sitting behind the partition. "I'm supposed to get bailed out shortly, so how exactly does that work?"

The officer was a pretty black woman who didn't appear nearly as annoyed with me as everyone else seemed to be. "Well, someone needs to post your bail, and then we will be notified, and you'll be released."

"Well, I'm positive that my bail has already been posted, so can you check in the system and see?"

"Name?" she asked as she wheeled the chair she was sitting in closer to her computer.

"Chelsea Handler."

"No bail has been posted," she told me after a couple of minutes. "That doesn't mean it hasn't been paid, but it's not in the system yet."

"Well, how long does it take from being posted to get in the system?"

"Sometimes a couple of hours, sometimes overnight. The system looks like it's down. You're definitely not getting out tonight. You better get yourself a sandwich before they run out."

I was unsuccessfully trying to fight back tears. I turned to leave and then walked back to the window. "Do you know where I can get some eyeshades?" I asked her.

"Eyeshades?"

"Yes. I need them to sleep. I am extremely sensitive to light."

"I don't know if they sell them at the commissary, but you can try. You need to have money in your account, which you don't have. Once you start working, you will be able to purchase stuff from the commissary."

That's where she lost me. I turned and walked toward the pay phone.

One woman was on the phone while another was yelling at her, "Get off that goddamned phone, you fucking bitch! Your five minutes is up!" The officer with the sandwich cart was passing by and threw three sandwiches in our direction. I caught one thrown in my direction, took one look at the white bread with thumbprints on it, and tossed it in the trash bin next to me.

"What the fuck you thinking?" asked the woman in front of me waiting for the phone as she ran over and retrieved my sandwich from the trash. "You can trade that for something." Then she handed it back to me.

"What can I trade it for?"

"Candy, soda, pills, whatever," she said. Finally, someone was speaking my language.

"What kind of pills?" I asked.

The woman on the phone hung up and the woman in front of me almost caught air lunging toward the phone. She picked it up and started dialing. I leaned forward and tapped her on the shoulder. "What kind of pills?" I asked again. She looked at her shoulder where I touched it and gave me a look that said any more contact with her would not be rewarded.

When it was finally my turn to use the phone, I made a

collect call to my aunt. My cousin Madison answered the phone, accepted the charges, and handed it to my aunt. I immediately started bawling. Being in jail was similar to being in a hospital bed: You're fine until you see or speak to someone from your family, and then you completely lose your shit.

"When are you getting me out?" I asked her.

"We're working on it. We had to put a lien on the house to get the money."

"What's a lien?"

"It's a loan, dipshit, against our mortgage," she explained.

"Oh, shit."

"It's fine, don't worry, we should have you out by the morning." Hearing for the second time in ten minutes that I would be spending the night caused the same sting that I felt hearing it from the officer behind the window, and a new rupture of tears exploded.

"Chelsea, are you okay?" my aunt demanded.

"No!" I wailed. "There are gangs here and people are trading sandwiches for tampons! It's complete chaos, and . . ." I took a deep breath. "And . . . ," I continued, "I'm sleeping in a bunk bed."

"Chelsea, just try and get some sleep. We will get you out of there as soon as we can. Dan's going to the bail bondsman first thing in the morning."

I used the sandwich I was holding to wipe the tears off my face. "Do not tell my father," I told her.

"He already knows," she told me. "He's fuming."

"Oh, no."

"Yeah, he's livid. He can't believe your sister is such a jackass."

"Oh, really?" I asked, comforted by this development.

"Yeah, he said he won't speak to her until she starts taking medication."

"Oh, wow."

"Hey, Smurfette! Get off the fucking phone!" a woman behind me yelled. I was so startled, I didn't even say good-bye or hang up. I dropped the phone, took my sandwich, and high-tailed it back to my bunk. I was much taller than Smurfette and preferred the Barbie nickname from earlier in the afternoon. It wasn't going to be easy to get any of these lunatics to take me seriously, but I was hell-bent on trying.

I climbed up on my bed and put my head down on the pillow, which had the consistency of a pancake. I placed my sandwich under it for extra support.

"You not gonna eat that?" asked a frosted blond-haired white woman in the top bunk next to mine, her mouth full of the sandwich she was already gnawing on.

"Do you want it?" I asked, jumping at the opportunity to make a friend.

"Shit, I'll take it," she said, and put out her hand. Her name was Lucille.

"What are you in for?" I asked her.

"Murder."

The notion that someone who used a fake I.D. was put in a bed next to a killer was not lost on me. What kind of operation were they running here? I suddenly realized that this was what people were referring to with the phrase "hard time."

I searched my mind for the correct lingo to converse with a murderer. "Who'd you knock off?" I asked nonchalantly, trying to hide my fear by picking in between my toes and then smelling my fingers.

"My sister, the cunt," she said.

"Really? I'm thinking about killing mine," I told her as coolly as I could.

"Yeah, sister was a cunt, slept with my man."

"Did you kill the guy?"

"Nah, didn't get the chance, would've though," she said as she piled my whole sandwich into her mouth in one sweep.

"Right." I nodded. I didn't want to pry, yet I wanted to know how this frosted-blond petite woman murdered her sister and where in her body she was storing the two sandwiches she had just demolished. She couldn't have weighed more than one hundred pounds and she was about five-foot-six. This woman/killer was a testament to my theory that the crazier you are, the more calories you burn. That's why psychos are always so skinny.

"The best sandwiches are around Thanksgiving. That's when they use the real shit," she said.

"Yeah, well, I'm not going to be here over Thanksgiving."

"Yeah, that's what they all say," she told me.

"No, really." I told her. "I'm Jewish."

"Lights out in ten minutes. Lights out in ten minutes!" someone announced over the loudspeaker. I hadn't gone to the bathroom since that morning before I got on the bus, and I knew I wouldn't be able to hold it in much longer. I had seen an open area that looked like a bathroom near the information booth, which I had made a personal pact with myself to try and avoid. I thought I could hold it if I didn't ingest any liquids.

"Do you want to go to the bathroom together?" I asked Lucille.

"Sure." She smiled. "I'll go to the bathroom with you. Ain't nobody gonna bother you."

"Oh, I'm not worried about that," I lied. "I play karate. I'm a black belt." I wanted to trust Lucille, but knew if she had turned on her own sister, the chances of her turning on me were pretty strong. I wanted her to know that if it came down to it, I could protect myself. "I've done time before," I added as we headed toward the bathroom.

"Yeah, where?" Lucille asked.

I searched my mind trying to think of another prison. "Alcatraz."

"Fuck."

"You don't know the half of it," I told her. There were a few stalls in the bathroom as well as some open seating, but I opted for some privacy. The first stall I walked into looked like someone had just had a miscarriage. I walked out and chose the next one. I peed for about three minutes straight and when I came out of the stall, Lucille was sitting on a toilet taking a dump.

"Hold on," she said with her teeth clenched. "I'm just finishing up." This was obviously how she stayed so thin: She immediately shit out any food she consumed.

"Hand me some toilet paper."

I grabbed some tissue and handed it to my new best friend.

After she wiped her ass, she pulled up her pants and headed back out to the main room. I wanted her to wash her hands, but didn't want to be bossy. "I'm just gonna wash my hands," I said, hoping she would take the hint. Instead, she took a menthol cigarette out of her pocket and lit it.

We walked back to our respective bunks and hopped in. I laid my head down facing Lucille, wondering if she was my prison soul mate. I was starting to understand the tales of lesbianism you hear on the outside. It made perfect sense that without any men around, women had only two options: weight-lifting or other women. I wondered if Lucille and I would have a wedding ceremony by our bunk beds or in the cafeteria. I would be so skinny by that time from all this self-starvation that I could probably fit into any gown my heart desired. Maybe Lucille and I could even fit into the same gown.

I wasn't really attracted to her, but I had on occasion slept with guys I wasn't attracted to, and figured there wouldn't be a huge difference. I stared at her as she mashed her cigarette out on the side of her bedpost. "So, how did you kill your sister?" I asked, trying to make small-talk with my future bride.

"With a hammer," she replied. "Took the bitch a good forty minutes to finally die."

I was not prepared for that response. My body immediately went into shock. It was everything I could do not to vomit. The only other time my body had this reaction was when I was ten years old and my next door neighbor pulled down his pants and showed me his penis. But even then, I was less taken aback. I leaned my head over the edge of my bed gagging, but nothing was coming out. I knew this was not the appropriate reaction to Lucille's declaration. I put my hand up to say I was okay until moments later, when I finally stopped heaving.

Lucille was sitting on her bed looking at me. I racked my brain trying to come up with an excuse for my reaction, but was so thrown off-guard, I just put my head back down on my pillow and said, "We should definitely keep in touch after I leave tomorrow." Then I rolled over and cried myself to sleep. I thought about how lucky my sister was that Lucille wasn't in our family. I wanted to hug Sloane tightly and tell her, "You stupid, stupid girl, do you know that under no circumstance would I ever hammer you?"

I woke up very early the next morning and opened my eyes. I looked around the room trying to think of a situation that could be any worse than this, and decided that the only thing that could be worse than prison was the navy. I looked over and Lucille wasn't in her bed. I grabbed my bag of toiletries and went straight to the bathroom. I had to pee and I desperately needed to floss.

Once I was done washing my hands, I heard my name being called over the loudspeaker along with five or six others. "Finally!" I exclaimed, and ran over to the glass booth, where a guard was waiting with a clipboard. I stood there while we waited for the other girls called to find their way over, thinking about how thin I felt. One more day of this, and my stomach would officially be concave. I loved it. Once the others arrived, the guard led us out a door, down a hall, and down two flights of stairs into what looked like a principal's office.

My name was called rather quickly and I went into the office, sitting down across from a Latino woman in her forties.

"Hi," I said, with a bounce in my step.

"Hi, Miss . . . Handler?" she said, looking up at me with what I took to be sympathy. Finally.

"Yup, that's me," I said, shaking my head at the injustice of it all.

"Okay, there are a couple of options. Do you have any special skills?"

"Skills? Not really, no. I'm good at reading, I can type pretty fast. . . . I'm not sure what you're asking me?" I asked, confused.

"Well, you're here for work placement, so there are different things to choose from: You could work in the kitchen, or you could work in the industrial shop, where you could make anything from license plates to wooden wind chimes, or you can enroll in school and get your GED."

"What are you talking about? No, no, no . . . I'm not working here, you don't seem to understand. First of all, I am supposed to be getting bailed out this morning. I do not want a job making wood chimes or fixing cars, and I already graduated from high school . . . barely, but I did, so I don't need a GED! I want to go home! I just want to go home! What exactly is the problem with you people?"

"Listen, Miss Handler, everyone thinks they are going home.

But the reality of the situation is that eighty-five percent of the inmates booked end up spending a minimum of six months here, and if you want to start earning money, the best thing for you to do is get a job."

That was it. I stood up and placed my hands on her desk. "Listen up, miracle ear," I told her. "I spoke to my aunt last night, and she has already paid the money to get me out, okay? I am waiting for them to release me any minute. That is the situation. So for all I care, you can put my name down to plant prison flowers, or style inmates' hair, or head up the women's fucking field hockey team. I am not staying here!"

"Next," she said as she shuffled some paperwork. I walked outside her office and sat down. I was incensed and I also really wanted my mommy. Why wasn't anyone getting the fact that I would not be taking up permanent residence in a women's prison?

I looked up at the ceiling. "Are you there, vodka? It's me, Chelsea. Please get me out of jail and I promise I will never drink again. Drink and drive. I will never drink and drive again. I may even start my own group fashioned after MADD, Mothers Against Drunk Driving, but I'll call it AWLTDASH, Alcoholics Who Like to Drink and Stay Home."

When we were taken back to the main room, there weren't many women there. Apparently it was breakfast time, but I opted to go back to bed. As I climbed back into my bunk, I wondered how much weight I had lost already. Would people even recognize me when I was released?

I daydreamed about what it would be like when my father

finally saw what my body had been reduced to; I even considered shaving my head for a more dramatic effect. "You have no idea what it was like, Dad. Some of the stuff . . . I just can't even say. . . ." I would take long pauses while looking down and shaking my head. I would imply that there was penetration, possibly sodomy, if not only to play the sympathy card for years to come, but also to remind everyone that my sister was an alien and needed to be excommunicated from our family.

I dozed off and was awakened moments later by Lucille smacking me in the face. "No! Noooooo!" I screamed.

"Your name. They're calling your name to be released."

My eyes lit up bigger than the first time I had seen Jon Bon Jovi perform live. I jumped off the bed and started to run toward the booth.

"Wait!" Lucille yelled. "Aren't you even going to say good-bye?"

I turned and ran back to give her a hug, but was dumbstruck when she planted her lips directly on top of mine and held them. My arms fell to my side and I waited for her to finish kissing me. There were hoots and hollers coming from the women around us, and one of them yelled out, "Hammertime's got a girlfriend! Hammertime's got a girlfriend!"

"I'll e-mail you," I said as I slowly backed away.

"Barbie's going home to her daddy," a large black woman with dreadlocks yelled as I was taken by an officer out of the room and downstairs to an outbooking room, where I was handed a bag filled with the clothes I had come in wearing.

Twenty minutes later I walked out the doors of Los Angeles

County Women's Prison, otherwise known as Sybil Brand Correctional Facility, into the bright sunlight. I wondered who exactly Sybil Brand was and who she had pissed off in order to have an entire women's prison named after her. I made a mental note to google her later.

I saw Lydia's car parked at the far end of a circular driveway. Upon seeing me, she and my friend Ivory jumped out and started running toward me with their arms outstretched, like a scene out of *Chariots of Fire*. "Thank God I'm alive!" I cried. "Thank God I'm alive."

The whole way to the car, Lydia and Ivory were telling me how horrible the past thirty-six hours had been for them and how they both had to call in sick to the restaurant where we all worked.

"Does everyone know I was in jail?" I asked.

"Yeah, Chelsea," Ivory said. "We got together a fund and everyone chipped in. Even Hermano the busboy. We were worried your aunt wasn't going to get the money fast enough, so we started asking everyone."

"How much did you get?" I asked her.

"Fifty-five dollars."

"None of us are ever driving drunk again," Lydia said. "We are all taking taxis from now on . . . well, for a while anyway."

"I don't want you guys to be jealous," I told them, trying to distract myself from the fact that they could only raise fifty-five dollars on my behalf, "but I've made a new friend and her name is Lucille. We've already kissed on the mouth."

"Oh my God," Lydia exclaimed looking back at me. "Were you raped?"

"Face raped," I proclaimed as I got in the passenger seat of Lydia's car. I wanted to get home as soon as possible and weigh myself.

I went to court about three months later, when I was given my sentence: five hundred hours of community service, a fine of twenty-five hundred dollars, and three months of DUI school.

My favorite of the three was DUI school. The instructor was a small Asian man who repeated one thing at the beginning and end of each class: Under no circumstances, when being pulled over by the police, do you admit to having had anything to drink. Advice I would have valued much more had I received it months prior to getting my DUI. But still I valued it all the same.

CHAPTER FOUR

Bladder Stones

I was visiting my parents in New Jersey for a three-day break during my first book tour, and I had just come from the car wash, where I had taken their minivan to be disinfected. My parents are two of the most unsanitary people I know. They will leave fast-food bags, soda cans, coffee cups, and perishable items in their car for weeks at a time. When my father picked me up from the airport, there was a half-eaten apple rolling around on the floor mat, a melted chocolate bar stuck to the passenger seat, and a small order of McDonald's french fries in the glove compartment.

"I have an idea, Chels," my father said to me as I walked in the door. "I think you should start your own clothing company but only design thongs and lingerie."

My sister Sloane was sitting on the couch playing with her new baby girl, Charley, while our dog Whitefoot looked on in disgust. With every baby my brothers and sisters had, our dog became more and more depressed.

"He's been talking about it for the last two hours," Sloane said as she rolled her eyes. "He also wants you to write on all the clothes 'I'M A CHELSEA GIRL.'"

"Whaddya think, love? We could really rake in the big bucks," my father went on. "You've got a great sense of style, and with a shape like yours, you could also model the stuff."

"Why would I design clothing?" I asked.

"Why would she design clothing?" he asked the air and then Whitefoot, as if the answer was so obvious, even the dog would know. "Why *wouldn't* you design clothing, is the real question. You've got a huge fan base."

"No, she doesn't," Sloane said. "Not big enough to launch a clothing line."

"A lingerie line, goddammit! A lingerie line!" he yelled.

My father is always yelling for no apparent reason. He yells at unsuspecting people all the time, but his favorite person to yell at is Sloane, who usually responds with a "what the fuck is your problem?" look.

"Calm down, Melvin," my mother chimed in, as she emptied an entire box of Carr's crackers into Whitefoot's bowl along with some freshly made egg salad. Whitefoot's "bowl" is a stainless-steel baking tray. My parents are under the impression that our dog is Edward Scissorhands and can somehow manage to put the egg salad on top of the cracker and enjoy it like a human.

"Don't give him the pepper crackers," my father said. "He

only likes the plain ones. The pepper ones give him gas."

I looked over at Sloane, who was rubbing her temples.

"Anyway, back to the thongs," my father continued. "We'll have your sister Sidney run the company—"

"Can you please stop using the word 'thong'?" Sloane said, with her eyes now closed. "How do you even know what a thong is?"

"Yeah, Melvin," my mother added. "How do you know what a thong is?"

"Oh, come on! Thongs are the new bloomers. What are you girls, living in the dark ages? All the girls are wearing them; Chelsea's been wearing them for years. Sylvia, I wouldn't mind seeing you in one," he said, looking at my mother with his bowling-ball head tilted to the side and an enormous grin on his face. Suddenly Whitefoot started to bark uncontrollably and run back and forth from the front door to the living room while we were seated.

"That's the mailman," my father said as Charley began to wail. "Whitefoot, quiet!"

"Ugh, that dog has some serious problems," Sloane said, as she picked Charley up. "You need to send him to a dog trainer."

"He has a little social anxiety, that's all. You don't send a ten-year-old dog to obedience school," my dad screamed over the dog's barking. "It's just not done."

"No, *you* don't do it," my mother said in her most argumentative voice, which is about a half an octave lower than her regular voice.

"The mailman comes here every day," Sloane said. "You'd think the dog would figure that out by now. He's so stupid."

"He's not stupid, he's just depressed! But he's a good Jewish doggy who's very loyal, isn't that right, Whitefoot? Goddammit, Whitefoot, come here and shut up! Sylvia, look and see if that's the mailman."

"No," she said, looking in the direction of the front door. "I don't think so."

"Dad, how are you supposed to fit 'I'm a Chelsea girl?' on a thong?" my sister asked him once Whitefoot also realized it wasn't the mailman and had quieted down.

"We'll put it on the front."

"And who's going to run this company?" Sloane asked. "JLo?"

"Nah, I don't like the stuff JLo's coming out with. Too trashy. Something a little more sophisticated. You and your sisters will design the garments and I will make all the executive decisions."

"Yeah, you seem to have created quite a prolific empire with your used-car company; the obvious next move would be to branch out into women's lingerie," I told him.

"There she goes again, beating up on her daddy. You hear this, Sylvia?" he yelled to my mother, who was standing three feet away, ironing a pair of my father's sweatpants.

"What are you ironing, Mom?" Sloane asked her.

"Dad's sweatpants," my mother said with a groan.

"Well, for Christ's sake, it's not slave labor. She likes it when I have the creases in the front."

"No, Melvin, I told you I would prefer you to wear slacks but you insist on wearing sweatpants, and if you're going to wear them, I at least want them to be ironed."

"I look good in sweats," my father proclaimed. "Besides, I can't keep my slacks on with this extra weight." The "extra weight" my father was referring to has been there for thirty years.

My two-hundred-fifty-pound father then proceeded to try and get up off the couch, which took three false starts. When he did get up, he called out to Whitefoot. "Let's go, Whitefoot, you wanna go to the bathroom?" He walked over to the sliding-glass door that leads to our backyard and went outside with Whitefoot. While the dog lifted his leg, my dad chose to simply face the woods and pee in our backyard.

"Mom, I don't want Charley to come over here if Dad is just going to pee anywhere he feels like it and then not wash his hands," Sloane said.

"He's got those bladder stones, Sloane. When he has to go, he has to go," she said.

"I understand that, but it wouldn't take him any longer to walk to the bathroom than it does to walk outside, Mom," Sloane accurately pointed out. My father complains about these bladder stones on a regular basis but refuses to get the operation needed to remedy the situation because it involves sticking a small tube into his penis.

"Just be happy he's not peeing in the driveway anymore, Sloane. It took me months to get him to go in the back. And to wear suspenders."

"The suspenders are an improvement, Mom," Sloane told her. "At least he doesn't walk around holding his pants up with his hands anymore. You have to make sure he keeps wearing them."

The problem with the suspenders my mother bought for him is that he hasn't adjusted the straps since he got them. So instead of attaching somewhere around his midsection, the suspenders clip onto his pants three inches below his nipples. Now picture the suspenders attached to a pair of sweatpants. This vision is what first led me to coin the term "camel balls."

My father came back inside and headed straight for Charley. "Hold up, Dad," Sloane interceded. "You need to go wash your hands. Pronto."

He looked at my sister as if she had asked him for heroin. My mother then took the spray water bottle she was using to iron and sprayed my father in the face. "Melvin, you know you have to wash your hands when the babies are here."

My mother likes to pretend that she's on top of the hygiene factor because my brothers and sisters are always dropping their kids off with her, but the truth of the matter is, my mother isn't washing her hands all that much either. My mother is European and likes to remind us of that every time any of us ask her when she took her last shower.

My father returned from the bathroom holding up his hands to show us the water dripping. "All clean." Then he came back and sat on the couch across from Charley, chanting her name but not pronouncing the letter *r*, so it sounded like

"Chahley." He does this slowly but loudly about fifteen times in a row at random intervals throughout the day while my sister sits with her eyes closed.

The phone rang and my mother looked around, startled, as if a helicopter had just landed on our roof. "Telephone!" my father yelled out. Not only can neither one of them ever find the actual phone, but on the rare occasion when they succeed, the battery is almost sure to be dead, or the answering machine has already picked up. I've never had a phone conversation with either one of my parents when the answering machine didn't pick up or I didn't hear static. "Where is the goddamned phone, Sylvia?" my father asked her.

"Look in between the cushions," my mother said, as she ran around the room like she was trying to catch a mosquito. "Here it is," she said, as she picked up at the same time as the answering machine. "Hold on," she told the person as I got up and unplugged the answering machine. "It's for you, Melvin; it's the manager at Shop Rite."

"Aha. This is Melvin. . . . Yes, sir. . . . Okay then. Very good." *Click.* The dial tone is the only indication to any caller (myself included) that the phone call is over. "All right, everything's all set. You have a book signing Monday morning at the Shop Rite," he said, looking in my direction. My sister started to perk up—she found this new development very amusing. Her eyes were still closed, but a large smile had emerged on her face and her shoulders were shaking.

"Now, how are we gonna get the books?" he asked.

"First of all, Dad, I'm not doing a book signing at a grocery store. Second, we can't just have the publisher overnight us books; it takes a couple of days," I told him.

"Well then, call Amazon," he said.

"You can't call Amazon, Dad, you have to order them online and it's not like they just hot-air balloon them over. Furthermore, I'm not signing books at a grocery store. Who's even going to show up?" I asked him.

"I'll print up flyers," he said, which caused my sister to spit up a little bit.

"Print up flyers?" Sloane asked him. "You can barely use the telephone."

"Where am I going to sign the books, anyway?" I asked. "In the produce section?"

"Really, Melvin, I don't know if that's really Chelsea's audience," my mother chimed in.

"What about the car wash?"

"No," I said.

"How about the deli?"

"No."

"I sold three at the Starbucks the other day."

"To who?" my sister asked.

"To customers, Sloane! Who do you think? I told them my daughter is a bestselling author and she's a graduate from Livingston High School and they should buy the book. I've been a salesman for forty-some odd years. You don't think I know how to move a couple of books?"

"Well, if you're such a good salesman, why don't you sell some of those cars in the driveway?" my mother chimed in.

My parents fight about two things: the ten to fifteen cars my father has had parked in the driveway for more than ten years, and his eating habits. My parents live in a nice neighborhood, and my father doesn't seem to understand why our neighbors are continually calling the police to report him for having too many cars in our driveway.

"Oh, here she goes," he says, looking at my sister and me. "Listen, right now my focus is on Chelsea and the book. I've got a lot of plans. How about doing a signing at Best Buy? God knows they've got the equipment for a speech."

"I turned to Sloane and asked her if she wanted to see a movie."

"Oh yeah," said Sloane, immediately perking up. "Let's go see *Mr. and Mrs. Smith.*"

"Excuse me?" I replied disgustedly.

"I'm dying to see that movie."

"If you think I'm going to go give those two homewreckers my money, you've completely lost your marbles. I will never go see another Angelina Jolie movie again."

"Oh, please," she said, groaning.

"Oh, please, nothing!" I told her. "I will not support the two of them. The only temptation, obviously, would be a third installment of *Lara Croft: Tomb Raider*. But I think I'll just have to cross that bridge when I come to it."

"Please," she begged, "I really want to see it."

"Absolutely not," I told her. "It's either happy hour, or we can go see *Herbie Fully Loaded.*"

"I'm not going to happy hour," Sloane said. "I have a baby."

My sister had been using this baby excuse ever since she had the kid, and it was starting to get on my nerves. "Oh, would you shut up with the baby already?" I said. "That's all you ever say anymore, as if you're the only one in the world who's ever had a baby. I could have a baby too . . . if I had gone through with any of my pregnancies."

"Chelsea," my mother said, with the same look she reserves for me whenever I tell my sister that the back of her baby's head is flat.

"I'll take a baked potato," my father blurted out, the same way an attorney would yell "objection" in a courtroom.

"Here, Melvin," my mother said as she handed my dad his freshly ironed yellow sweatpants. "Please put these on."

"And not out here," Sloane added.

"Aren't there any regular pants you can put on?" I asked my dad. "I really don't think sweatpants are a good look for the outdoors. Especially on you."

"They're the only thing I can fit into right now, love; why can't you just accept your daddy the way he is?"

"Because, you're not the biggest man on the planet, Dad. There are other men who seem to find pants that fit them."

"What if I wear a tie?" he asked.

"Sloane, dear, how about some fresh grapes?" my mother asked in a voice more appropriate for a six-year-old.

"I'll take some grapes," my father called out. You'd think my father was stapled to the couch the way he barks out orders, but the simple truth of the matter is that he's entirely too top-heavy to make a clean sweep from the sofa to the kitchen without knocking something over.

My mother walked over with a bowl full of grapes and handed a bunch to my sister, who then inspected them like she does every piece of food—as if there's anything that could stop her from inhaling it.

"What is it?" my mom asked, as Sloane made a face at her grapes.

"Nothing," Sloane said, pulling what looked like a dog hair off the top of her bunch with disgust and then popping one after another into her mouth.

In between bites of his own, my father plucked a grape and attempted to throw it into Whitefoot's mouth. Instead, the grape hit the sideboard, ricocheted and bounced off the side of Charley's head and right into Sloane's eye.

"Ow! Dad!" Sloane yelled out.

My mother once again reacted like there had been gunfire and dropped the bowl of grapes on the floor. "Melvin, what the hell is the matter with you?" she said in her feeble version of yelling as she hurried over to my sister's rescue.

"Bad doggie!" my father yelled, as Whitefoot ran over to eat all the grapes that had just fallen to the floor.

"Sorry about that, Sloane. I was just trying to give Whitefoot a grape," my father said as he winced at his misfire. "Goddammit, Whitefoot, why didn't you catch that grape?"

"Are you okay, darling?" my mother asked, cuddling Sloane like she had just fallen off the monkey bars at the playground.

"Look at that faggot," my dad motioned as some guy promoting exercise equipment came on the television screen.

Whitefoot started barking again.

"Sylvia, look and see if that's the mailman."

She walked from the kitchen into the living room and looked out the front door again. "Yes, I think so."

"Okay, I gotta go talk to him about Sloane's diet," he said as he got up and almost fell over.

"Is the mailman moonlighting as a nutritionist?" I asked Sloane, who was now eating grapes with one eye shut.

"You're gonna like this one. Dad told me that he would pay for me to go on NutriSystem. He said it would be my birthday gift because it's kind of expensive. So, after he convinced me to do it, which I wasn't all that excited about in the first place, I went online, picked out thirty days' worth of meals, which took about an hour. Then I punched in Dad's credit card number. And it was declined."

"What does that have to do with the mailman?" I asked her.

"His theory," my sister explained, "is that the mailman's mad because Whitefoot barks at him, and so in retaliation, he takes some of his mail and throws it in the Dumpster at the post office. That's why the credit card company didn't get his payment."

"Well, that seems like a logical explanation. Is that where you think the rest of the bills he never pays on time are?"

"Dad is very good at paying his bills," my mother added. "Sometimes they're late, but he always sends them."

"I don't doubt that he sends them, Mom," I explained.

"My point is that there usually has to be money in the account for the check to clear."

My father walked back in the living room and sat down. "Guy's a deadbeat. Sylvia, remind me to go down to see the postmaster tomorrow."

"I'm going home," Sloane said, shaking her head.

"Well, I'm coming with you," I said. I needed some one-on-one time with my niece to ensure that my sister Sidney did not secure the favorite aunt position. All my brothers and sisters live in New Jersey and I live in Los Angeles, so I constantly have to fly from coast to coast in order to make my presence known to my nieces and nephews.

Sloane wanted a baby for a long time and it took her three years to get pregnant. She's one of those people who has wanted a baby her whole life. Meanwhile, I'm on the Internet investigating tubal ligations and researching how to bring on early menopause. I don't want to permanently tie my tubes, but I want to prevent any further accidents. I'm interested in something more temporary—like a slipknot. I know having a baby is a huge responsibility. It's at least a five-year commitment, and I would be silly to think I was ready for it.

After she had her baby, Sloane was the happiest person in the world. "You will do things for a child that you would not even do for yourself," she told me over the phone a couple of weeks after she had Charley.

"That's totally how I feel about midgets!"

"I think they prefer to be called little people," she said.

"Well, Sloane," I told her, "you've obviously never hung

out with one, because I know from personal experience that they either like to be called 'midget,' or 'little fucker.'"

My sister handed me Charley as she started packing up her baby items. She was on her way to the front door when the phone rang again, which I ran over to answer before another Hiroshima ensued. It was a call for my father about one of the cars he had listed in the paper. He is frequently advertising the cars in our driveway, and has been fielding inquiries about them my entire life. He has the phone manners of Saddam Hussein, and instead of being civilized while trying to lure a potential buyer, he interrogates them about their salary, nationality, and religion. He hung up the phone and met my stare. "Change of plans. Chels, I'm going to need a ride. I got an Oriental who wants to look at the Mustang."

My sister looked at me and smiled. "I guess I'll see you tomorrow."

"I'll drive," he said, as he put his hand out for me to help him get up.

"Dad, this better not take four hours," I told him.

Growing up in our house, my brothers and sisters learned quickly that "a ride" could take anywhere from two hours to two days. My father has cars parked all over New Jersey. Some are parked at office buildings, some at private businesses, some are at the local high school. He once parked two of his cars in a family friend's driveway for two months while he was in the hospital having a bone marrow transplant.

"Well, I'm going to take a nap," my mother said, as she put my dad's baked potato in a bowl and headed upstairs to take one of her three naps per day. Apparently the two telephone calls had taken their toll.

"What are you doing with my baked potato?" my father asked, standing there aghast.

"You can't eat a baked potato while driving," she responded, and turned the corner.

We headed outside to the minivan and got in. "Put your seat belt on," I told him.

"Can't. Won't fit."

My father refuses to wear a seat belt, and I can't think of anyone whose driving skills require it more. I reached over as he raised his hands in the air and I strapped him in. I looked in the backseat and saw a box of my books that my father had purchased at Barnes & Noble.

"You know it's illegal to resell books you buy at Barnes and Noble, right?"

"That Charley is something, isn't she? What a girl! What a girl!" he said as he ran a stop sign. "Sloane really loves that little girl. She really loves her."

"I should hope so. She's her daughter."

"And you're *my* daughter, and I'm very proud of you. You got a lot of chutzpah. You know where you get that from? Your daddy."

If you don't respond to my father, he will continue as if you're waving your hand to say "Keep going!" It is very important to interrupt him before gets on a roll.

"Where are we going?" I asked him.

"Newark. We gotta pick up the Mustang. It's parked at the

DMV, and then we'll show it to the Oriental and move it to a lot in West Orange. I got a *schvartzah* at the DMV, big woman."

"Huh?"

"She helps me flip titles, helps with registration, nice lady, black as night, though, and she's got a *tuchas* the size of midsize sedan."

"What does she get out of the deal?"

"What does she get out of the deal?" he asked. "I bought her a watch from Costco, that's what. You know, Orientals are cheap. They don't want to spend a lot of money. Car's listed for $2,235 in the paper and that's what I intend on getting. Mileage is a little high, but it's got A/C and tires. Even had the floor mats washed."

"How many miles does it have?" I asked him.

"120,000," he said as he changed lanes without signaling.

"Does this car have airbags?" I asked, looking around for mine.

"The reason I listed it for $2,235 is tricky," he went on. "If you put an odd number for the price, that will catch the eye more than say, $2,200 even, or $2,240. An odd number will stand out much more than an even number."

"Well, what happens when they actually see the car?" I asked.

"Well, they either take it or leave it. They get one shot!" he said, pointing his finger in the air. "Some people want to think about it," he said, making air quotes. "That means they're not interested and they're liars. Not serious about buying a car, just trying to waste my time. If the person's gonna buy the car, they're gonna show up with cash like I tell them to, and decide right on the spot. There's no time for dillydallying." While my father gave me those details, a guy in a convertible Jaguar we had just cut off was laying on his horn while simultaneously giving us the finger.

We finally arrived at the Department of Motor Vehicles in downtown Newark, where my father headed toward the back corner of the parking lot to collect his gold 1990 Ford Mustang with tinted windows.

"Is that a bullet hole?" I asked, noticing what looked like gunfire on the passenger-side door of the Mustang.

Melvin stopped the car and sat there looking at his seat belt like he had no idea how to unbuckle it until I leaned over and pressed the button to release it. "Gotta warm up the car. Give me a couple of minutes and then follow me," he said as he hopped down from the minivan. Following my father in a separate vehicle is not dissimilar to playing *Pole Position*. He will go through yellow lights, leaving you to either run a red light or lose him completely, only for him to call you from his cell phone minutes later asking you where you got your license.

I followed him to a Wendy's parking lot, where he parked the Mustang and got out. Motivated by pure boredom, I decided to go to the drive-through and get some chicken nuggets. After ordering, I pulled around to the window to pay and found my father standing there telling the woman behind the window that he wanted a cheeseburger. The lady was trying to explain to him in broken English that he needed to be in a car to order food, when I interrupted and told him to take a hike. "You're not having a cheeseburger, that's the last thing you need."

My father looked at me, looked at the woman through the window, turned, and walked back to the Mustang. Soon after, the Asian who had called about the car pulled up in a black Honda Accord with his son and parked next to the Mustang. They got out of their car and spoke for a couple of minutes with my father before getting into the Mustang to take it for a test ride. This I had to deduce on my own, because it would never occur to my father to come over and tell me he would be back in a couple of minutes.

Just as they were pulling out of the parking lot, the car stalled. My father got out after a couple of seconds and popped the hood. I was watching this circus from inside the minivan while chewing on a chicken nugget, wondering what my father thought he was going to find under the hood. He's not a mechanic. Unless the problem was something as obvious as the battery not being attached, he wouldn't be able to fix a car if his life depended on it. He leaned in under the hood for a couple of seconds and then walked around to the driver side, where the Asian father was seated, and gestured with his thumb for the man to get out. Surprisingly, my father hopped in and was somehow able to start the car. He got back out, shut the hood, and walked back around to the passenger side.

I sat alone in the Wendy's parking lot for about forty minutes until I was joined by a homeless woman with full eye makeup wearing a cape. The driver-side window was only open a crack and I was too lazy to turn the engine back on to lower it. "Here." I took one of my chicken nuggets and squeezed it through the open part of the window. My calculations were off, and instead of the nugget fitting perfectly through the quarter-inch opening, it ended up losing its breaded coating on its way out. She took the chicken nugget, looked at it, and then slammed it on the ground. I understood that the nugget had lost some of its appeal in the transfer, but was a little alarmed at her reaction. I was, after all, sharing. We stared at each other for a full minute before I reluctantly took a dollar out of the consul and shoved it through the window.

"Good luck with everything," I yelled as she walked away without saying "thank you."

I retrieved my eye shades from my purse, reclined my seat, and fell into a light slumber until I heard the car door open and saw my father grabbing one of my books out of the Barnes & Noble box. "Make it out to Quan," he barked, and handed me a Sharpie.

He took the book and walked back over to the Asian man and his son. They looked over with big smiles and waved. Then the man took some money out of his pocket, handed it to my dad, and got into the Mustang while his son got into the Honda and drove away.

"How much did he pay for the car?" I asked as I pulled out of the parking lot.

"You must be a good-luck charm, love," he said, patting my leg and then taking out a wad of cash. "Nice guy for an

Oriental—had to negotiate a little bit, but he ended up buying the car after all. And he bought a book!"

"How much did he pay for the car?" I asked as I moved my leg away from his hand.

"Asking price was $2,235. I gave it to him for $2,225. But I made $5 on the book. Charged him twenty bucks for that. I paid fifteen bucks for it at Barnes and Noble," he said, as if I didn't know how much my own book cost.

"Let's take the girls out to dinner and celebrate," he said. "Call your mother and tell her to meet us for dinner."

"She said she was taking a nap," I replied.

"She'll be up by now, and call that Mormon sister of yours. She won't turn down a meal. And don't miss the goddamned light!" he yelled as we approached an intersection with a yellow light.

"Goddammit, Chelsea!" he screamed when I did the unthinkable and decelerated instead of stepping on the gas and gunning it through a major intersection in a minivan at ninety miles an hour. "This light is a disaster. We could be here for hours." Then he opened his passenger-side door, got out of the car, turned his back to me, and peed in the middle of the street.

CHAPTER FIVE
Big Red

After sleeping around for the better part of my twenties, it somehow occurred to me that I wasn't giving everyone a fair shot. There were men I'd encounter who I wouldn't think twice about having sex with based on their appearance alone. I knew that if I ever had a chance at becoming a respectable ambassador for countries such as Uganda, Kazakhstan, or the Tropic of Cancer, I would really have to be more of an egalitarian. I had slept with a handful of black boys in my late teens, and knew that I would have to open my borders even further in order to be taken seriously by any third-world government. It was time for a redhead.

Along with the 97 percent of women who can see, I have never been a fan of redheaded men. First of all, I am unclear as to why they are called redheads when, for the most part, their hair is bright orange. Obviously, bright orange–head doesn't roll off the tongue the same way, but in all honesty, it should either be "orange-head" or "Hawaiian Punch–head."

For a woman, being a redhead is a completely acceptable trait. Oftentimes it can be extremely attractive. Conversely, being a redheaded man is pretty much a lose-lose situation. It's incredibly hard to take redheaded men seriously, never mind think of them in any sort of sexual capacity. Obviously, it's not their fault that they were born with red hair. However, it is their responsibility to change that hair color once they have access to a convenience store or supermarket. It's one thing to have a harelip, or even a leg that's a couple of inches shorter than the other, but if you're a man with red hair and don't opt to do everything in your power to alter that, then obviously you're not serious about experiencing all life has to offer.

My theory on the redheaded race is that they have no positive role models paving the way for them. It's not like Ronald McDonald or Carrot Top have really helped their cause. Who are they supposed to model themselves after? Danny Bonaduce?

I did not set out to find a redhead; I was fortunate enough to have one come my way. My manager, Dave, had called to tell me a screenwriter he knew was coming to see me do stand-up. He was interested in basing a character on me in his new film. My manager didn't mention that this guy had red hair, which I think would be a fairly reasonable thing to mention, especially if his hair took up more square footage than a Mini Cooper.

His name was Austin, and he introduced himself to me after I performed at a bar on Sunset that has since changed names four times over. Austin was about six-two with a completely beautiful body. He was really muscular—and not in a ripped, infomercial kind of way. He was built, but softer. I liked his body instantly. His head was a completely different story. "How," I wanted to ask, "could you think that a bright orange Afro was acceptable?" It looked like he had gone bobbing for apples in a barrel filled with Fanta orange soda.

Despite his appearance, he was seemingly coherent as we made introductions and then took a seat at the bar. I kept waiting for him to stutter or have a bout of Tourette's—something to back up his decision to leave the house in what could have very well been a clown's wig. But there were no such symptoms. He was perfectly normal, bright, and chivalrous. He pulled out a bar stool for me, asked me what I wanted to drink, and ordered.

He was cute in a way. And the more I talked to him, the more I found him attractive for having enough confidence to walk around with a lid like that.

Now don't get me wrong, I have some very serious shortcomings of my own. I know that I have a tendency to drink heavily at night. I know that my body, specifically my midsection, has trouble staying where I put it, and I also know that I am pretty much useless when it comes to TiVo or anything involving road maps. I've learned that on both of those fronts, it's just better not to get involved. But most important, I know that I don't want anyone to ever look at me and think, *What the fuck happened to her hair?*

Austin and I proceeded to knock back a couple of Ketel

One and grapefruit juices, which happened to be my drink of the moment. Someone told me that grapefruit was a great detoxifier and I decided I wanted to start cleaning out my liver *while* I was having a cocktail. I liked that Austin didn't just order a beer of some sort, or, God forbid, wine. There's nothing more annoying than a man ordering wine at a bar when you're not eating.

Doesn't everybody know that wine is supposed to go with food? I've never in my life finished a long day of work and thought, *Gee whiz, I can't wait to get my hands on a bottle of lukewarm Cabernet.* I have a bunch of girlfriends who love wine and I've never really been able to relate. I mean, yeah, maybe if you're stranded on an island and the only other option is coconut milk. Or if it's a really nice bottle of wine and you're having a really nice meal. Other than that, I don't see the point. I'd rather have water. And by the way, I'm not a huge fan of water, either.

After our third drink I learned that Big Red knew people from my high school. That was certainly a red flag, considering I didn't remember having any actual friends in high school. I had a couple of girlfriends, but no one who I thought would have anything positive to say about me. I didn't really spend much time with anyone my own age during high school because I believed my true calling would be representing New Jersey in the U.S. Senate, and if that didn't work out, I could always fall back on becoming an Olympic pole vaulter.

I thought I was completely too cool for my classmates, and

couldn't comprehend how they could hang out at malls on the weekend. I much preferred spending romantic weekends in Hoboken with my twenty-one-year-old accountant boyfriend who would wine and dine me at T.G.I.Fridays. I had no involvement with any extracurricular activities at school, mostly because the one time I tried out for cheerleading I was summoned to the nurse's office the next morning to be tested for scoliosis.

Sometime after our fourth Ketel One and grapefruit, he mentioned that he was going after Shannen Doherty to play the lead in his movie and was finding her extremely difficult to deal with. "Yeah, no kidding," I told him. "Everyone knows that."

By the way he reacted, you would have thought I told him that slavery never happened. He laid into me with the same gusto as a right-wing political pundit on the *O'Reilly Factor* defending President's Bush right to vacation six days out of the week.

His insane passion for a person who not only starred in a television show about witchcraft but also worked at a place called The Peach Pit intrigued me to no end. I love people who have such passion for complete nonsense. When I told him that most people are well aware of the fact that she's difficult to work with, he launched into a promotional campaign with a fervor I hadn't seen since Anna Nicole Smith signed with TrimSpa.

According to Big Red, Shannen had been through a very traumatic childhood, beginning with a role on *Little House on the Prairie*, then moving on to that other show with Wilford Brimley. The *Little House on the Prairie* part I totally understood; if I had to go without TCBY or Donkey Kong Jr. when I was a child, things would have probably ended up a lot differently for me. Who knows what kind of long-term effects milking an animal while wearing pigtails can have on a little girl. But Wilford Brimley? How anyone could have anything negative to say about Wilford Brimley was borderline preposterous.

"All right, now you've crossed a line," I told him.

After two more cocktails I called Home James, a drunk-driving service that sends someone over to where your car is located, with a scooter that folds up into your trunk. They drive you home, take their scooter out, and then hightail it back to headquarters. It's not cheap, but it's definitely a great way of avoiding Jack in the Box. They charge you extra to stop for fast food.

Just as I got into bed, my cell phone rang and it was Austin. He asked me if I had gotten home okay and then asked me if I thought we'd ever have sex. "Wow, that's pretty straightforward. I like your style," I said. "But I doubt it. . . . I'm kind of seeing someone," I told him. Saying I was seeing someone wasn't a complete lie, since I was kind of casually sleeping with a guy named Darryl who lived in my apartment building—but it wasn't anything I would have mentioned had Austin had a more reasonable hair color.

"Kind of seeing someone, or seeing someone?" he asked.

I have to admit I was turned on by his drunken confidence,

which I knew was drunken because it hadn't been there until he went on his Shannen Doherty tirade. "Well, kind of," I replied.

"Okay, well, I'll call you tomorrow and see if you change your mind."

"Tootles." I hung up and wondered why I would say something so stupid when I clearly had the upper hand. It was so like me to be sitting at a poker table, holding a royal flush, only to have another player at the table catch me high-fiving myself.

I woke up the next morning and stared at my ceiling, wondering why Excedrin couldn't just walk out of my bathroom cabinet, hop onto my bed, and triple-axle its way into my mouth. Then my thoughts turned to Big Red. There was something about the way he helped the guy from Home James fold up his scooter and pop it into my trunk that was very endearing. Then my thoughts moved north to his hair, and my body shuddered. If only it wasn't so bright.

My manager, Dave, called me later that morning to see if Big Red had come to my show.

"Yes," I replied.

"And?" Dave asked.

"And what?" I asked.

"Well, did you discuss the movie at all?" he asked me.

"No, Dave, as a matter of fact, we didn't. And you could have mentioned his hair."

"I think he's pretty cool," he responded. "He actually just wrote a movie for a client of mine and he's a real stand-up guy. He's the type of guy I would like to see you end up with."

"Really?" I asked. "He's the type of guy you'd like me to end up with? An orange-head?"

"He's really smart, Chelsea. I think he went to Stanford," Dave said.

This statement turned me on the most because I was definitely at a place in my life where brains were starting to matter. There are only so many conversations you can have about NASCAR and female mud wrestling before your mind starts playing tricks on you.

"Well, who knows if he'll even ask me out?" I said coyly.

"Chels, I got another call," he said. "Is there anything else?"

Not exactly the response I was looking for.

"Thanks for nothing," I said, and hung up.

I wondered how long I would have to wait for Big Red to call me.

I rolled over and picked an *Us Weekly* magazine off the floor. The cover had a picture of Angelina, Brad, and their little Eskimo son, Maddox. I sat staring at the photo, wondering why this little guy looks so pissed off in every picture.

At first I thought he was just pissed about his mohawk, but then I realized he's probably furious. Maddox must have thought he hit the jackpot when some A-list celebrity rescued him from third-world Cambodia, only to discover that she was going to shuffle him back and forth to *every* other third-world country in the universe. He's probably like, "When the fuck are we gonna get to Malibu, bitch?"

My phone rang and I jumped out of my chair with an

alacrity my body hadn't seen since a tetherball class I had taken in the fall of '94. Unfortunately, the number that came up was Darryl's, the guy I happened to be sleeping with who lived down the hall. He was going away for a few weeks to shoot a movie with Hulk Hogan, and was calling to ask if I would pet-sit his goldfish while he was away.

"You mean you're not bringing him with you?" I asked.

"It's actually a girl," he said.

"Oh. Yeah, I guess I can watch her."

He hung up, came over, dropped off a key, and told me where the fish food was. Why anyone without children would have a fish was beyond me, but what's even more alarming was that Darryl's fish's name was Maude. I had learned this information once before, but somehow had managed to block it out.

Then he asked me if I wanted to come over and play Ms. Pac-Man. He had one of the real arcade versions in his apartment.

"Sure," I said. "Maybe we can use this opportunity for Maude to really get comfortable with me," I told him. I knew Ms. Pac-Man was code for getting naked in the middle of the afternoon, but the only thing on my calendar that day was an appointment with a palm reader, which wasn't until 5 p.m.

Darryl and I had a blast together. We'd have crazy rabbit-like make-out sessions, and then I'd make fun of him for his receding hairline. Darryl was the epitome of a Hollywood actor—he had been in a ton of B-movies and was absolutely, madly in love with himself. It was fine, because he knew he was ridiculous, and we would actually have a lot of laughs making fun of him together. He would stand naked and recite monologues to me, all the while asking me to confirm his suspicion that he was one of the most underrated actors working. I would tell him again and again that if he would just consider getting hair plugs, he would get the recognition he deserved.

Two days later in Darryl's apartment, while feeding Maude, my cell phone rang and it was Big Red.

We chitchatted for a minute or two before he asked me if I was happy to hear from him.

"I guess," I responded dryly, not really sure how one responded to that line of questioning.

"Try to contain your excitement," he replied. "It's a little overwhelming."

"I'm sorry, I'm fish-sitting and the fish doesn't look good. She's upside down and not moving. Is that how they sleep?"

"Does it plug into an outlet, or is it battery operated?" he asked.

"The fish?" I asked.

"Yes," he responded.

"I would assume it's battery operated since I don't see a plug, which, by the way, would be really dangerous, considering it lives in water."

"Good observation. Sounds to me like she's dead."

"Oh, that's just perfect," I said. "I've only been fish-sitting for two days, and I already killed her?"

"What kind of fish is it?" he asked.

"I don't know. The orange kind."

"A goldfish?"

"Yeah, that's it. It's a goldfish."

"Well, just go get another one. They all look the same."

"How much is that going to run me?"

"I think they're like a dollar," he said.

"That's a little more than I wanted to spend."

"So, anyway," he said, changing the subject. "I decided I want to take you to dinner."

"Oh, really?"

"Yep; I'll pick you up tomorrow night around seven." This turned me on immensely, and at the same time sounded to me like false arrogance. Like a guy who was trying really hard to pretend he wasn't insecure. I didn't let that overshadow my decision because either way, I love a man who takes charge. But I also didn't want to seem too eager.

"How do you know I'm available for dinner?" I asked. "I'm a very busy girl."

"Are you busy?"

"Not really."

"Good, see you tomorrow," he said, and then he hung up on me.

Whether it was organic or forced, I was extremely attracted to Big Red's take-no-prisoners approach. My mind quickly raced toward the future and I wondered what it would be like to have redheaded children. I had the same fears interracial couples must have when deciding what society's effects might be on a child of mixed race. Would they be discriminated against because of their hair color? Never mind the cluster of freckles that would accompany that color of hair and the incessant teasing they would have to endure, being compared to Connect the Dots or, God forbid, Lindsay Lohan.

I looked down at Maude again and decided to leave her in her bowl until I found a replacement for her. I thought it would be in everyone's best interest that I wait until the day before Darryl was supposed to return to buy a new fish. That would leave a very small window for me to commit another homicide.

I was very much looking forward to my date with Big Red, but also scared that when I saw him sober I might not be attracted to him. Obviously I would need to drink heavily before my pickup time.

Three weeks and about eight dates later, Big Red and I decided it was time for penetration. I was very surprised to find myself becoming more wildly attracted to him every time I saw him. Each date we went on, his hair became less and less of a focal point.

I didn't intend on waiting a certain amount of time to sleep with him, but since he knew my manager, and since I was technically sleeping with Darryl, who was still away shooting his movie, I decided to behave somewhat respectably. Obviously a threesome would be out.

What I was completely astounded by was the fact that Austin was packing some serious heat. Not only did he have a huge penis, but he was great in bed, and another added bonus: He had extremely sensitive nipples. I had never met a man with such sensitive nipples before, and took enormous delight in the fact that the minute I touched one, he would climax. I wanted to thank the person responsible for inventing the nipple and applaud them for creating such a great addition to the human form. Who knew nipples could be so much fun? With that knowledge in hand, sex never lasted a second longer than I wanted, and I considered this to be the jackpot of all jackpots.

The part that wasn't a jackpot was his baseball mound of red pubic hair that looked like it had literally been attached with a glue gun. I couldn't believe how much there was, and wondered how he had never heard of scissors, or—more appropriate for that kind of growth—hedge trimmers. I didn't understand what porn he was watching to not be aware of the trimming that was happening all across the world among his compatriots. I'm not a finicky person when it comes to pubic hair maintenance and I certainly don't expect men to shave it all off, leaving themselves looking like a hairless cat. That's even creepier than seeing what Austin had, which could really only be compared to one thing: a clown in a leg lock.

Obviously, at night it was much less offensive because I couldn't see the seriousness of the situation, but in the daylight, between the boldness of color and the length, I was quite taken aback.

Even though Big Red would vacillate between being shy and overconfident, in many ways he was growing on me. One minute he would say something like, "I can't believe you're even dating someone like me," and the next minute he would tell me he had plans for the weekend and wasn't sure if he could squeeze me in. I told myself that maybe he was trying to play it cool in order to land the account, and I found him even more charming. I even considered cutting Darryl out of the picture if things kept on going with Red, but I didn't want to make any hasty decisions.

I hadn't seen Darryl in a few weeks, but knew that once he came back, we'd be back to our same story. It was an affair built on convenience, and neither of us ever pretended that it would lead to anything of significance. We both knew that if someone else came along we would go our separate ways with no hard feelings. Our relationship was the equivalent of a reach-around: It felt good in the moment, but once it ended, it would be easily forgotten.

My aunt Gerdy called and asked me to bring the redhead over for dinner. Gerdy and her husband, Dan, are both huge boozers, and happen to hate each other. Somehow during their twenty-five year union they managed to have nine children and buy a house in Bel-Air. They have three dogs, seven birds, several fish, a hamster, a gerbil, and no cleaning lady. Their house is not dissimilar to a zoo, but with more animals and no one to clean up after them.

Once when I was babysitting for my manager's son, Luke, he wanted me to take him to the Los Angeles Zoo for the day, which ended being the worst idea ever, mostly because the Los Angeles Zoo is the lamest zoo in America. First of all, they have no animals. From what I can remember they had maybe half of a giraffe and a mosquito. After the zoo Luke was still asking to see animals, so I took him to Red Lobster and told him that we were at an aquarium and to stare at the tank. When that didn't work, I brought him to my aunt's house, which kept him occupied for four hours. To this day, he still thinks her house is the real zoo.

Gerdy's a great cook, a great mother, and a great aunt, but as far as sharing information with her that you wouldn't ever want repeated, you're better off confiding in Linda Tripp.

I didn't know if it was such a good idea to bring Red over because my aunt can be a total bitch, but I did think it would be a good opportunity to score a fish, since Darryl was coming home the next week. I warned Austin about my family and told him he shouldn't feel at all like he had to go, but he said he'd love to.

The thing about my aunt is that she only spills her guts when she's drinking. I always convince myself that if I tell her something while she's sober, she might not remember it when she's drinking. But I have learned the hard way that the opposite is actually true: She gets drunk, somehow manages to paraphrase my words exactly, and then promptly forgets everything she said the next morning when you confront her. In addition to that, she frequently orders things online in her state of inebriation, which would be fine except that one morning, a small black boy from Angola arrived at their front door holding a case of Viagra.

My uncle Dan has problems of his own. He has never made a drink or cooked a meal for himself, and I'm convinced that the only reason they continued to spawn children was in order to have a twenty-four hour bartender. Every single morning,

Dan wakes up, walks outside in his bathrobe to get his paper, and then plops himself on his toilet to read it while taking a shadoobie. And every morning while he's doing this, his parrot, Henry, mimics the phone ringing. This has been going on for close to ten years, and without fail, each morning my uncle gets up off the toilet with his boxers around his ankles to answer the phone, only to realize it was the bird. "Goddammit, Henry!" he screams day after day. "Goddamn birds!"

Inside a half hour of meeting Big Red, Aunt Gerdy pulled me aside and reminded me that I hadn't been sure whether or not to go out with him based on his hair color, and that, initially, she had thought I was overreacting. However, upon meeting him, she completely understood my dilemma. This assessment would have been fine had she not walked right outside to the table where Red was sitting with all nine children and my uncle and said, "Jesus, Austin. Chelsea wasn't sure about you in the beginning because you're a redhead, which we all thought was so ridiculous, but now seeing it in the broad daylight, I totally understand where she was coming from. Do you put something in it to make it that bright?"

"Oh, goddammit, Gerdy," my uncle said. "Go back inside and have another drink."

I don't remember much more of that night, because immediately following my aunt's little speech, I headed straight for the wet bar, where I did three shots of Jose Cuervo straight from the bottle. I know it was exactly three because in my head I counted three solid beats while the bottle was lifted to my beak. I also remember grabbing a snifter from behind the bar, walking over to my family's fish tank, and scooping out the first goldfish I could get a hold of.

I walked into the kitchen and found my aunt emptying an entire brick of cream cheese into the pasta she was cooking. "That's nice," I said. "Thanks for being so nice to Austin. I'm sure he'll look back at this evening as one of the best nights of his life," I said, holding the fish in the snifter. "I'm taking a fish."

Gerdy walked over to a drawer, pulled out a Ziploc bag, and handed it to me. "You might want to put it in this. And don't let the kids see. I think that may be a new one."

I took the Ziploc bag and slipped it over the top of my snifter, sealing it around the stem of the glass. I looked up and saw Gerdy shaking her head.

I walked outside and put the fish in the cup holder of my car.

The rest of the night was cloudy, but luckily my aunt passed out shortly after she served dinner, and my uncle took that opportunity to perform his daily ritual of apologizing up and down for my aunt's behavior. Austin didn't seem too bothered, and he and my uncle got into an hour-long conversation about golf.

Austin wasn't being overly affectionate with me, but come to think of it, he really never had been. Then he made a comment about my nine-year-old cousin that I felt was completely inappropriate. My cousin Rudy is a little hyper. We're all pretty sure my aunt drank during his entire pregnancy because she drank through all of her pregnancies, and for the most part all the kids turned out okay. Physically, anyway. Rudy's eyes are a little uneven, and one isn't always looking in the same direction as the other, but I didn't think that was grounds to ask Gerdy if he had Down syndrome. Cerebral palsy maybe, but Down syndrome was just flat-out uncalled for.

I apologized for my aunt's behavior and admitted that, even though I was a little shocked by his amber waves of grain when I met him, his hair had really started to grow on me. We didn't have much to say to each other on the way home, mostly because I was trying to balance the Ziplocked snifter glass in order to avoid having the new fish jump ship. When we got home, we jumped into bed and both passed out before anything could happen.

In the morning, I woke up to see him getting dressed, and shut my eyes to avoid catching a glimpse of his pitcher's mound. When I thought it was safe to open them I did, and there was definitely some awkwardness. He kissed me good-bye and told me he'd call me. I looked over at the snifter on my nightstand and couldn't help thinking that the fish and Austin had the same exact hair color.

I got dressed and took the new fish, which I secretly decided to name Lawrence, over to Darryl's apartment. When I got to his place, there was a slight problem. I realized that Maude was about three shades lighter than Lawrence and about two inches shorter, which, for a goldfish, is pretty extreme. I thought that if I sullied the water a little more, the murky hue could potentially discolor Lawrence, and maybe his skin tone wouldn't be so bright. Since I was not exactly sure how to soil fish water, my thoughts moved to disposing of Maude. I took a tablespoon out of Darryl's kitchen drawer and used it to transport Maude from the fishbowl straight into the toilet, where I promptly flushed her. I went back to my apartment, changed into a leotard, and decided to watch a workout video. I always make it a personal rule to get familiar with the tape before I actually join in. This would be my fifth viewing in the span of a month, and I was almost ready to participate.

Five days later, I still hadn't heard from Austin. I called my uncle and he told me that I was better off without Red.

"Why?" I asked.

"Well, he doesn't really seem to have much of a personality. I said hello, and the guy was stumped for an answer."

"What are you talking about?" I asked him. "You were talking to him all night."

"Yeah, well, I was trying to be polite, but it wasn't an easy conversation. He's not for you. Let's put it that way. He doesn't have much to say."

"Well, you'd be quiet too if you went over to someone's house for dinner and the host's opener was, 'Your hair looks stupid.'"

"Well, that couldn't have been the first time he's heard that, Chelsea."

"Good-bye," I said, and hung up. I called my friend Ivory and discussed it with her.

"I'm surprised you even care, Chelsea. It's not like you were going to marry the guy."

"Well, yeah, but I didn't want to hurt his feelings. That's just mean."

"Well, that can't be the first time he's had his feelings hurt. Not with that Afro."

"Jesus! Can't anyone get beyond his hair?" I asked her.

"Chelsea, if you really think that's the reason he hasn't called, then why don't you call him and apologize?"

"No, what if he's trying to blow me off?"

"Maybe he is."

"Well, I am not about to go make an appointment to get dumped."

"Well, then shut up, and go visit Darryl."

"I can't. He's on location filming a movie with Hulk Hogan." Ivory hung up on me without saying good-bye. She seemed to be doing that an awful lot, and I must say that I respected her for it on some level.

I felt like a loser. No one likes getting blown off, and unfortunately for me, this wasn't my first time. I thought about calling him, but wouldn't even know what to say. Obviously he had no interest in talking to me. If a redhead could dump me, who knew what was next?

The next day, Darryl called and told me he was on his way home from the airport and asked if I wanted to go paintballing. "Not at all," I told him, "but you should see Maude. She is getting so big!"

"What? Who?" he asked, confused.

"Your fish, Maude. She's gotten so big. I went to the fish store and found all these great vitamins to make her color more electric and to help her burst into womanhood, and I have to tell you, it's like they worked overnight." I figured that any adult with a desire to go paintballing would have no trouble believing that there were growth hormones available for goldfish.

"Wow," he said. "That was really thoughtful of you. I didn't even think you liked fish."

"Well, that's ridiculous." I snorted. "Who doesn't love fish? They're so . . . crazy."

Later that night, Darryl came over to my apartment with pictures of him and Hulk Hogan on the set of their movie. Darryl barely recognized Maude when he first saw her. "She looks amazing."

"I know. She's so much more . . . upbeat," I said. "It's amazing what a couple of vitamins can do." I needed to change the subject. "So tell me about the Hulk. How long does it take for them to make his whole body so green?"

"It was Hulk Hogan, Chelsea. Not the Incredible Hulk."

"Right. That's what I meant." Even though the last thing I ever thought would turn me on in the way of copulation would be a picture of Darryl being headlocked by Hulk Hogan, I needed confirmation that I was attractive on some level, and decided to face rape him. Just as we were rolling onto my bed and Darryl was getting ready to mount me, my doorbell rang.

I walked out of my bedroom to the front door while fixing my clothes, and opened it to find Big Red.

"Oh my God!" shot out of my mouth before I could stop myself. "Hi." Then I said it again. "Hi."

"Can I come in?" he asked.

"Oh, sure," I said, without moving.

"Are you going to move, so I can come in?"

"Yes, but I have to go to the bathroom," I said, and grabbed my vagina dramatically to look convincing. I walked back into my room as calmly as I could and shut the door.

"Get in the closet," I told Darryl.

"What?"

"Do it!" I whispered as loudly and as violently as I could through clenched teeth.

"Fine," he said, and walked toward the closet, which was filled with cardboard boxes. It didn't take long for both of us to realize there wasn't enough room for a car seat, never mind a full-grown human.

"Shit," I said, looking around the room for other alternatives. "Get under the bed."

"Oh my God." He slid underneath the bed, grazed his forehead on the frame, and rolled his eyes at me.

"Thank you," I said, and turned to leave the room. Austin was standing at my bedroom door when I opened it and he scared the shit out of me. "Aaaah!" I screamed. "You scared me!"

Big Red smiled and walked over to the chair in front of my computer, turned it around to face my bed, and sat down. "You're probably wondering why I haven't called," was his opener.

I ran over to my bed, sat down, and made as many adjustments to my seated position as necessary to completely dislodge the comforter and have it land on the floor to hide Darryl's naked body. Once I had accomplished the task at hand, I met Austin's quizzical gaze.

"I'm sorry, I have ringworm. Anyway, what did you want to talk about?"

"Ringworm?"

"Yup."

"Don't you get ringworm from dogs?" he asked. "You don't have a dog."

"You can also get it from fish," I stammered.

I coughed loudly after saying this in hopes of moving the conversation forward.

After a moment, he started. "Well . . . I mean, I really like you, Chelsea. I think you're really fun, and you're smart, and you're pretty . . ." Normally, I would have interrupted this terrible cliché of a breakup, but I knew that as long as he was talking, it meant he couldn't see Darryl.

"I just have to be honest with you," he went on. "I feel like maybe we are getting really serious in a short amount of time and I don't know if I feel comfortable with that. I have a lot of opportunities right now, and I don't want to be nailed down to one woman."

The fact that Austin was telling me that he had other opportunities while I had another guy under my bed was ironic. It's not like we were in some serious committed relationship. Yes, I liked him, but he was acting like I just told him I wanted to have his orange babies.

"What are you talking about?" I asked him.

"Well, I mean, your family was great and everything, but I don't think I'm ready to be in that serious of a relationship." The idea that Red thought meeting my drunk aunt and uncle meant that we were on the brink of getting engaged was ridiculous. I understand that meeting someone's family usually means you're taking the relationship to the next level, but not with my family. Obviously, if I was serious about having a relationship with someone long-term, the last people I would introduce him to would be my family.

"Chelsea, I just think maybe you're taking this relationship a little too seriously."

"How many times do you think you can use the word 'serious'?" I asked him, trying to restrain myself from standing up and strangling him. "I think you're being a little dramatic."

"Well, I had a feeling you would be upset and take this badly."

"Okay, you know what, Red? I am not upset about you breaking up with me. Well, it is kind of shocking, but the fact that you are being so dramatic about it is quite alarming. This is hardly a serious relationship."

"Fine," Austin said. "Intense might be a better word. Things have gotten a little intense." This is when I blew a gasket.

"Intense? Intense?" I yelled. "You want to talk about intense? Try dating three guys at the same time. I'm trying to remember names and keep secrets and shit!"

I don't know why I said "three," when actually I had only been dating two people. I quickly invented a third person in my head to back up my story. I decided his name would be Luther and he would work with animals. Who did Big Red think he was? And who did he think I was? I felt like I had been doing *him* a favor.

He stared at me, apparently shocked by my outburst. "And by the way," I added, "you really think highly of yourself." I wanted to add something about his hair, but decided to leave that to the next girl he dumped. "Please go. I have a date with a very dynamic zookeeper that I do not want to be late for."

Red got up and walked out of my bedroom toward the front door. Before he made it out I added one last thing: "And you might want to think about trimming your bush!" Then I ran back into my room before he could say anything about my beaver and slammed my bedroom door. I knelt down on the floor and lifted the comforter up as Darryl rolled out from under my bed.

"Ha ha!" Darryl sang as he crawled out. "You got dumped! I don't know which I liked better, the rash or the zookeeper. That guy was a moron. Could you imagine anyone being that clueless?"

I tried to keep a straight face while wondering if Big Red could ever be convinced that his pet had tripled in size over a two-week period and had brightened its skin color by taking fish supplements. Darryl and I started laughing so hard, we were crying. The fact that we were laughing at two different things was a perfect summation of our relationship.

"You want to hear something really funny?" I asked him in between snorts. "Maude died."

"What?"

"Maude, your fish." I took another deep breath in order to get the sentence out without guffawing. "She's dead and I got that new fish from my aunt Gerdy's house." Then I went into another fit of hysterics, except this time I was laughing alone.

"How could you do that and not tell me?" he asked, instantly sobering up.

"What?"

"Chelsea, I've had Maude for six years."

"Well, I'm sorry. It's not like it was intentional. I tried to revive her, but she was out like a light."

"It's not funny, Chelsea. This is not funny at all." Darryl was on his feet and getting dressed.

"Oh, Jesus," I said, now feeling like a complete asshole. There's nothing worse than ruining a perfectly good moment by thinking someone else will find humor in something they absolutely do not. "I can't believe you're really upset about a fish."

"It's the principle. I trusted you to look after Maude."

"Yeah, and obviously you made the wrong decision. You know I don't particularly like animals, especially ones you can't tickle."

Darryl stormed out of the apartment while I sat on my bedroom floor, dumbfounded by the day's events. I picked the phone up off the floor and called Ivory.

"Big Red broke up with me."

"Why?" she asked.

"Because he thought I was getting too serious."

"Well, that's absurd; you couldn't even have sex with him during the day."

"I know, and then Darryl stormed out because his fish died on my clock."

"Huh?"

"I was babysitting for Darryl's goldfish and the little hooker went belly up on me."

"Why does Darryl have a fish?" she asked.

"Exactly my point!"

"Why didn't you just get him a new fish?"

"I did, but it was a few shades darker and a little longer and after Big Red left, we were laughing so hard, I thought he'd think it was funny too."

"Why was Darryl there when Big Red dumped you?"

"He was over when Red showed up unannounced."

"So Big Red broke up with you in front of Darryl?"

"No, asshole. Darryl was under the bed."

The next sound I heard was a dial tone.

This had been a day full of rejection, and frankly I was pretty sick of it. I wanted to experience unconditional love without the hassle of getting a dog or giving birth. It was clear that this was a turning point in my life. I logged on to AOL.com and Googled "hunger." It was time to adopt a baby. Two, maybe, depending on how expensive they were.

CHAPTER SIX

Dining in the Dark

I had finally received the paperwork confirming my adoption of two children from overseas. One was a nine-year-old girl from Guatemala and the other was a thirteen-year-old boy from Zimbabwe. The even better news was that they didn't come to live with me right away. I would just be paying for their food, clothing, and books for school. Once they turned eighteen they would be allowed to visit if we both agreed on meeting. I was, of course, invited to visit them at anytime, but Guatemala and Zimbabwe weren't exactly on my top ten countries to see list. I was looking at both of their solemn faces in the pictures they had sent, pleased that I had done exactly as I set out to do when buying my kids online—picking the two who looked the most upset.

I decided right then and there to call them both Earl.

The phone rang and it was my U.K. publisher calling to

ask me if I would be interested in crossing the pond to do a little press for my book's British release date. They told me my services would be needed for a period of ten days in February, which luckily happened to be one of the eleven months I had absolutely nothing planned workwise. "Bloody hell," I told them in my best Madonna impersonation. "I'd love to."

I called my friend Sarah, who had just been broken up with by her Cuban fiancé, and was the one person who needed to get out of the country faster than my cleaning lady. Sarah and her fiancé had dated for seven years, and two weeks before the wedding he decided to tell her he wasn't in love with her. Coincidentally, he had realized this after sleeping with a waitress who worked down the street at the International House of Pancakes.

Watching your friend get news like that and seeing her go through the emotions of canceling a wedding—and the life she thought was going to come along with it—is heart-wrenching. All you want is to be able to fix it, but you and all your friends are completely helpless. It was the night of her breakup that I vowed never to have children, for fear one of them might be a girl and get broken up with. That's why I turned to adoption.

"Wanna go on an all-expense paid vacation to London?" I asked when she picked up the phone.

"Yes, let me just quit my job."

It upset me that I was going to have to desert my children so soon after acquiring them, but truth be told, I was exhausted. Motherhood was no joke and neither was lying awake every night wondering where in the hell they were and if they had been able to score some rice that day. The bottom line was that Mommy needed a break. My next step was to get an all-clear from my OB-GYN to travel abroad.

Once we got to London, I realized that going on vacation with Sarah was slightly more enjoyable than getting a glass eyeball installed. She had more energy than the Energizer bunny and was in nonstop planning mode, toting printed-out itineraries, maps, charts, color graphs, and recommendations for what we would do each day. There was shopping and museums, we had to go to Parliament, Bond street, Piccadilly Circus, Cambridge, and then the London Eye. The trip was turning into a full-blown nightmare, and it finally occurred to me why her fiancé had broken up with her: He was probably scared to go on their honeymoon.

The thing about Sarah is that she can be a lot of fun to be around. She's smart, she's funny, she drinks like a fish, but she has way too much energy for someone without a crystal meth addiction. She's one of those people who should either be working on a campaign trail or running a wild animal park.

"Hey, asshole," I told her. "This isn't a scavenger hunt. You need to relax. All these activities are making my head spin. Can't we just go to a pub and get some bloody fish and chips?"

After only three days in London, I was hell-bent on using all of their colloquialisms, partly because I love English accents and all the phrases, but primarily because it was driving Sarah nuts. She didn't believe that "cheers" could actually mean "hello," "good-bye," and "thank you," so I spent every waking moment saying it to anyone and everyone we came in contact with. It didn't even have to be someone I was having an exchange with. I would just say it to people we passed on the street, in the park, lifts, loos, lorries. What pissed her off even more was when people responded in kind, which was almost automatic. "Cheers," along with "bollocks," "blimey," and "rubbish" became my go-to phrases in response to almost anything. It only stopped when we came home after a night of heavy drinking and ordered room service at two in the morning.

When the food arrived, I took it upon myself to scream, "Bollocks!" as I opened the door.

After the waiter regained his footing and collected our burgers that had been strewn all over the hotel's hallway like shrapnel from a pipe bomb, I ended up giving him a hundred pounds as compensation for scaring the living shit out of him.

The next day, after promoting my book on some woman's show who is supposed to be England's version of Oprah, but in much less expensive clothes, my publicist informed us that we had the night off to do as we pleased.

"I've already made reservations for us," Sarah informed me.

"There's a surprise."

Sarah had made three copies of my press schedule prior to even arriving in London. One for her, one for me, and one for the concierge at our hotel.

"We're going to Dans le Noir. It's going to be great," she told me. "You eat in the dark!"

"Why?"

"Apparently, it's huge in France, and it's supposed to heighten all of your senses. Being unable to see, the food and conversation take a much more prominent role in your dining experience. Your ears and taste buds go into overload."

"Are you reading that straight out of the Zagat guide?" I asked her. "Because you sound like an asshole."

"Chelsea, it's dining in the dark! Haven't you heard about this?"

She hailed a cab and twenty minutes later we pulled up in front of a restaurant that looked like it wasn't finished. Once inside, we were in what appeared to be the front room of the restaurant. There was a bar with a bartender behind it and three misplaced cocktail tables that looked like someone had thrown them into the room and left. Two homosexuals were sitting at one of them, and a large transsexual-looking black woman was sitting alone at another. An unbelieveably annoying French maître d' took our coats and greeted us unctuously. "Ladies! Welcome to Dans le Noir, vat is the name on ze reservation and vould you like ze key for your lockehhhr?"

"Our locker?" I asked him, confused. "Are we at the YMCA?"

"Ze lockehhhrs ah for your sha'kets and valubellz. Yu are not to bring anything into ze dining area!" he told us, rolling every *r* and overly dramaticizing every *z* and *s* sound. I had been there for five minutes, and I had already lost my appetite.

"We're not even allowed to bring our purses?" I asked him.

"No, that iz vat ze lockehhhr is for. Here iz your key. Zen you come back and peek a look at ze menu."

I rolled my eyes, handed Sarah my coat and purse, and headed toward the bar. "Triple Ketel One on the rocks, and lemons." Any true alcoholic who's been to London knows that getting drunk there is nearly impossible, due to the bartenders using an exact measurement of one ounce of alcohol per drink. It's no wonder everyone there drinks Guinnesses. In the midst of explaining to the bartender that "triple" meant "three," Sarah interrupted me.

"I don't think that maître d' likes us."

"No one likes us, Sarah, we're American. Everyone hates us."

"Right," she concurred, and ordered herself a triple Bombay martini dry. I grabbed a menu and flipped it open. "Wow," I said. "Look at the choices. There's either 'Duck' or 'Surprise'."

Those were the two things listed on the menu. "Duck," and underneath it read "Surprise."

Don Juan DeMarco came over and explained that we could choose one or the other.

"That's quite a selection," I said, handing him the menu. "I'll take the surprise."

"Do you ladies have any allergais?" he asked. "Ve must know before preparing ze food."

"Yes," I told him. "I'm allergic to duck."

"Aaaah, zank you, and you, madame?" he asked, looking at Sarah.

"I'll take the duck."

"Okay, ladies, you vill be seat-ad in just a few momenz." I couldn't help thinking that this man was faking his French accent. No one in his right mind could take himself seriously enough to talk in such an affected manner.

We sat at one of the tables in the front room as the door next to the lockers opened and what appeared to be a blind waiter peeked his head out and called for the two gay men who were sitting at one of the other cocktail tables. They got up and walked over to the waiter, who turned and with his back facing them, took the first man's hand and placed it on his own shoulder, leading him into an abyss of darkness.

"This is ridiculous," I told Sarah, watching them.

"I'm getting scared," she said, wide-eyed and giggling like a schoolgirl.

"Aren't you happy Albert called off the wedding? Otherwise we'd never have had the opportunity to dine at Dine la . . . what the hell is the name of this place?"

"Noir. It's Dans le Noir. He's such a scumbag. I hope he catches herpes from that waitress," she said.

"He will," I assured her. "And when she dumps him on his Mexican ass, I hope he loses his job and then pulls a hamstring."

"He's Cuban, Chelsea."

"Whatever."

"Do you think she'll break up with him?" she asked me.

"Yes, I do. He's a loser, and by the way, he's shaped like a woman. He's got a woman's ass."

"Really?"

"Yes, he has a woman's body, and with time, it will become increasingly more and more bitchlike."

"He did kind of have man boobs," she said.

"Sarah, they were bigger than mine. He's got to be at least a D-cup."

"Oh my God, he did. And by the way, he wasn't that good in bed either."

"Of course he wasn't, Sarah. Bitch tits can't be good in bed. It makes you feel like you're hooking up with another chick."

A waiter opened up the door to darkness and spoke a few words before the maître d' waved us over. "Mademoiselles, I do hope you enjoy Dans le Noir," he announced as creepily as Willy Wonka introducing all the Oompa Loompas to his guests at the chocolate factory. "Bon appetit."

Our waiter, who was clearly blind, and looking to my left while talking to us, introduced himself as Brian. He wasn't French, but he did have an accent of some kind that was extremely hard to pinpoint because he had the same pitch as Michael Jackson. Sarah, at this point, was of course brimming with excitement. Not only were we about to dine in the dark, but there was a real live blind man about to escort us into our bad dream.

"Put your hand on my shoulder," he said as he turned on his heels and led us into a dark corridor. Thinking that sounded a lot like a song lyric, I put my hand on Brian's shoulder, Sarah put her hand on mine, and Brian led us into what may have well as been a well. Not only was it pitch black, but I had no sense of anything around me and was relying on a blind man who had the voice of a four-year-old girl.

"Are you having fun yet?" I called over my shoulder.

"Oh my God, oh my God, Chelsea, I can't see," she whispered, squeezing my shoulder.

"Just take it nice and slow, ladies," Brian said as he led

us toward voices and clanging noises. "Okay, just take deep breaths if you feel overwhelmed."

"You're starting to sound like a porn director, Brian."

"Okay, girls, here we are," he said, ignoring my comment as he led us to our chairs. "The table is right in front of you."

"Thank you, Brian. I would have never figured that out," I told him, putting my elbows on the table and spreading my legs apart like a trucker. If no one could see me, I was going to take full advantage of it and break all the table manners I had grown bored with. All I was missing were a toothpick and a walkie-talkie.

Brian took our drink orders and left us alone. There were voices near us but none directly next to us.

"Chelsea, I'm getting really claustrophobic."

"Just breathe."

"I am," she said, clutching my hands, "but this is freaking me out." She was giggling, but in a very passive-aggressive way, and I wasn't sure if there was going to be some sort of full-blown panic attack.

"Sarah," I said sternly, "the lights are off, that is all. Just keep breathing in through your mouth and out through your ass."

"I'm hot."

"Drink your water," I said, feeling around for any water and knocking the silverware onto the floor in the process. "Here."

"I think I need to take my sweater off."

"So take it off."

"I can't," she whispered. "I have nothing on underneath."

"Sarah, no one can see you here, who cares? Take it off and rest your tickets on the table. I'm thinking about pulling my pants down just for shits and giggles."

"I think I may need to take it off, Chelsea. I think I'm hyperventilating."

"Take it off, Sarah, please, I do not want you to hyperventilate," I pleaded, and then got up and felt my way over to her side of the table. "Do you want me to pour a glass of water over your head?"

"No, no, I'll be fine," she said, taking deep breaths. Once her sweater was off, she started to calm down. Brian walked over to the table.

"It's me," he whispered. "Is everything okay?"

"Yes," Sarah told him. "I'm just a little claustrophobic. Can I get some more water?"

"And can I get some more Ketel One?" I added. "Are you sure you're okay?" I asked Sarah.

"Yes, I'm fine, go sit down."

"Sarah?"

"What?"

"If you had to have sex with the mâitre d' for two hours missionary style, or you had to go down on Star Jones for half an hour, who would you choose?"

"The mâitre d'."

I found my way back to my seat just as Brian came back and put his hand on my shoulder. "Hi," he said, "it's me."

"I know."

"I'm putting your vodka on the right," he said, maneuvering

my hand to touch the glass. "And Sarah, I'm going to put your water on your right as well."

Ten minutes later Brian came back and seated two English girls next to us. One of them was very sweet, but the other one didn't seem very interested in mingling with Americans. I got this impression right after I said "Hello," and she muttered, "Great, bloody Americans."

I am very sympathetic to why foreigners think that Americans are loud and obnoxious. Many of us, including myself, are. But just because we have a president who can't spell "cat" doesn't mean we all voted for him. Along with a huge constituancy, I am also counting the days until Barack Obama or Ryan Seacrest takes over.

The nice girl asked us if this was our first time at the restaurant, and how we had heard about the place. Sarah jumped in and told her all about her online research and how the restaurant originated in Paris, blah, blah, blah. The nice girl seemed a lot like Sarah as far as research and planning goes, and when it's coming from someone not so close to you, it can be more charming. I reminded myself to tell Sarah this in a private moment later.

Sarah told the girl that we absolutely loved it here and were having the best time in London. "What a great city you guys get to live in," she said, panting excitedly.

"Yeah," I said, trying to get in the conversation.

This is when the mean girl decided she would add to the conversation.

"Yes, it's nice being exposed to civilization, isn't it?"

Before I could respond, Brian walked over and leaned down above us. "Hi. It's me."

"Yes, Brian. We get it. It's always you. I'm me and you're you."

"Ladies, I apologize, but I am going to have to ask you to put your sweater and pants back on."

"What?" exclaimed the mean girl sitting on my right. "What are you, a couple of lesbos?" she screeched in her thick British twang.

"No," I told her. "We're not lesbians. We were hot and my friend was hyperventilating. We didn't think anybody could see us, considering it's pitch black in here."

"Do girls from your country have any manners?" was her next question.

"You know what, mean girl?" I said. "You are not a nice person. You should be a little more open-minded and not judge people based on what country they're from. I'm not asking you why all the men in your country refuse to get circumcised, am I?"

"Oh, that's lovely," she replied.

"No. Actually, it's repulsive. They look like fucking aardvarks, and I really don't appreciate it," I said, getting up from the table and squeezing myself back into my jeans. "Sarah, can we go now?"

"Yes," she said, and then screamed, "Brian! It's us!"

Three minutes later we were in the front of the restaurant opening up our lockers. We paid our bill with the mâitre d', who refused to make eye contact with us. Obviously, he had caught wind of our undress and found it very disappointing. "Au revoir," Sarah said as we walked out.

"Cheers," I added in as volatile a way as I could muster. "Can we please just get some fish and chips?" I asked Sarah.

"Your zipper's down," she said, shaking her head and then stepping into the street to hail a cab. "When did you take your pants off, Chelsea, and why?"

"I was doing it to support you! It was a sympathy disrobing."

"Oh, that's actually nice, thank you."

"Don't mention it," I told her as I turned my hand upside down and put out my middle and index fingers. "Low two?"

"No thanks." We hopped in a cab and Sarah told the driver to take us to any place that served fish and chips.

"There also needs to be a bar," I chimed in.

"Yes," she agreed. "A restaurant that serves fish and chips."

"I'm starting to become embarrassed about being American," I told Sarah. "I feel like our only real saving grace is the Olsen twins, and what does that say about us as a whole?"

"Not a lot. Do you hate Americans too?" she asked the driver, who looked more Pakistani than anything else.

"No, of course not," he told us. "Only the loud ones. Very good tippers."

"Yes," I agreed, pulling out my wallet and handing him twenty pounds.

"You might want to wait until the ride is actually over," Sarah said. "And don't you think twenty pounds is a little excessive for a five-minute cab ride?"

"If the only way for these people to like us is to buy their respect, than that is what I intend to do."

"That's very honorable, Chelsea."

"I take you to Fish Central in de Barbicon," our driver informed us in his Pakistani accent.

"Cheerios," I told him. "Word to your mother."

Sarah and I walked into the restaurant and were seated in the back, next to an older couple. "I want a cigarette," she declared.

"You don't even smoke," I responded.

"Well, everyone else is smoking, and it would be nice to just fit in after the day we've had. I don't understand. Everyone's been so nice up until today, and then it seems like everyone we talk to hates us."

"You know what makes no sense?" I asked her. "We have more foreigners in our country than anyone, and we don't treat them like that. I would never be mean to someone who was visiting America."

"Yeah, we let everyone in our country. I mean, we complain about the people who can't drive, but that's about as bad as it gets."

"And the people who own Seven Elevens," I added. "But aside from that, I find myself to be very open-minded."

"I really want a cigarette."

"Well, don't ask anyone here. They'll just get mad at us for bumming one cigarette and blame our homeland."

"You ask someone," she said. "I'm not in the mood to talk."

I looked over at the older couple sitting to our right, who

were both smoking. In my best British accent, I leaned in and asked, "Could I bum a fag?"

They were very nice and handed me one, which I handed to Sarah. "Thanks," she said to the couple, and then leaned over. "I was too shy to ask for it myself."

I looked at her, wondering what was the point of me asking for a cigarette if she was going to talk to the people anyway. Twenty minutes later, I was looking at her, wondering why we were still talking to this couple. And further, why I was being forced to continue speaking in a ridiculous English accent.

"So where exactly did you grow up?" the man asked. "You have such an interesting accent."

"Yes," Sarah chimed in, smiling, "it's such an interesting story, tell them."

"Well," I began, searching my brain for something moderately plausible. "I was born in Devonshire, and my parents split up when I was five, when I moved to a little town called Lewisham, which is in South London." The only reason I knew about Lewisham is because I had an ex-boyfriend who was from there and we had gone to visit his mother years earlier. It was the only outskirt town I really knew anything about.

"I'm very familiar with Lewisham," the gentleman responded. "Which part did you live in?"

"Yes, Chelsea, which part?" Sarah asked.

I wanted to bitch-slap Sarah. Why was she continuing on with this when I was doing her the favor in the first place by bumming the fag? If I knew these two were going to become our new best friends, I would have spoken normally.

"Well, I don't quite recall—I only lived there for a few years—but it was right across the park from Whiteheath." I couldn't remember the name of the street, but remembered there was a huge park across from a more upscale town that I thought was called Whiteheath.

"Do you mean Blackheath?" the man asked me.

"Righty-o! That's it, I knew I was a bit off." His wife and Sarah laughed as if they were on my side, but I could see the guy's eyes growing more skeptical, and the questions wouldn't stop.

"And then where did you live?" was his next question.

"When I was eleven, I was flown to a boarding school in California and I spent the next seven years there."

"Bloody hell," he said. "Well, how did you manage to keep your English accent?"

"I dated an English guy," I told him. "He was pretty much the only person I talked to."

"When you were eleven?"

"Oh, God no!" I blurted out, forgetting that had been the age I mentioned. "I was twelve when we started seeing each other."

"Can I have another cigarette?" Sarah asked the woman.

"Really?" he asked me, with an overexaggerated question mark on his face. "Lewisham is kind of a working-class town. How were your parents able to afford such an education?"

I didn't appreciate the rapid-fire style in which he would shoot one question after another at me, or the inappropriateness of his inquiry into my divorced parents' income. That was none of his business, and it was clear that he did not grow up with the same etiquette that had been instilled in me by my English nun/auto shop teachers, or whoever was in charge at the boarding school I had never attended. I started to chew my fried cod slower and slower in order to give myself more time to come up with reasonable answers to my interrogator's questions.

"Well, I got a scholarship, actually."

"How fascinating," his wife added. "So interesting." I could tell she truly did believe what I was saying by her sincerity and good-heartedness, which shone through with every smile. He, on the other hand, was trouble.

"What kind of scholarship?" Hitler asked.

I knew my response had to be sharp and I wasn't about to blurt out something ridiculous. After some consideration, I responded.

"Bowling."

"Bowling, bloody hell? I didn't even know you could get scholarships for that!" he wailed. That was when Sarah realized she needed to come to my defense.

"Oh, in the States, yes! It's hugely competitive, and Chelsea is one of the best."

"Enough about me," I said. "How did you two meet?"

The woman, Anne, went on to tell us that she used to be a groupie of his band and they'd been together for twenty years. Sarah asked them what band he was a part of, and he said, "You've probably never heard of us, but we're called the Eagles."

"Shut up!" Sarah exclaimed. "Of course we've heard of you!" Even I, whose music library consists solely of Whitney Houston's and Hilary Duff's greatest hits, knew the Eagles were a big band. I couldn't believe we were talking to Don Henley and his wife.

They went on to regale us with stories of touring through New Zealand and Ireland and of all the crazy drugs they had done, and parties they had gone to. I, of course, loved this part of the conversation, and asked them very pointed questions about the various strains of Ecstasy they were able to get their hands on. More important, the minute I heard the word "Ireland," I needed to find out everything I could about leprechauns, but I knew that would be a hard word to say in a fake English accent. I was mouthing it silently to myself for several seconds until he asked me if I was okay.

"What are those tiny little green men called?" I asked.

"Frogs?"

"No, the ones that live in Ireland."

All three of my companions looked at me, concerned, until Sarah came to my aid. "She likes little things," she informed them. "She's talking about leprechauns."

"Anyway," he went on, "we fell in love, managed to stay in love, and here we are today, past our prime, but happy as two clams at a swap meet."

Sarah was practically drooling every time the guy opened

his mouth. She couldn't believe that we had run into such an icon at some random fish-and-chips restaurant. "This is so crazy!" she repeated, over and over and over again.

"Do you have any children?' she asked them.

"No," they responded. "How about the two of you?"

Sarah said no, and I was about to do the same until I remembered that I did indeed have two prides of joy.

"I do," I told them. "I've got a nine-year-old and a fourteen-year-old. Different fathers."

"What are their names?" the wife politely inquired.

"Earl . . . and Earl."

Sarah interrupted me with more questions to him about all the awards his band had won and all the hit songs they've recorded. He was very flattered and downplayed everything. He was humble, and it was charming.

I was relieved that the attention had shifted from me, but was also regaining my confidence and wanted to give my accent another shot without talking about my personal history.

"So let me ask you," I interrupted. "What is it like having to compete with all these other Brits who seem to be stealing your thunder. Amy Winehouse, Lily Allen, Shakira."

"Can we get the check?" Sarah yelled to our server across the restaurant.

"Cheers," I told them both as we got up to leave after paying our bill in a flurry.

"Cheers," they said and kissed Sarah good-bye. They awkwardly smiled at me and opted for a handshake. Then Don handed Sarah his card before we walked out the door.

"You should write fairy tales," Sarah said, wrapping her scarf around her neck. "I have no idea why you write real stories when you've obviously got an imagination on par with J. K. Rowling."

"I prefer to think of it as quick in a bind."

"No, Chelsea, quick in a bind is when you have to make up something fast. Your lies are completely unnecessary and, above all, ludicrous. Some of the things that come out of your mouth have never even crossed my mind."

"Why would they cross your mind, Sarah? I'm the one who's thinking them."

"It's truly fascinating," she said. "I think there's a pretty strong chance you could be a full-blown sociopath."

"I wouldn't argue that," I replied.

Sarah took the card Don Henley had give her out of her pocket and squinted while trying to read his name. "Chelsea, what does this say?"

"What?" I asked, leaning in to look at it.

"Does this say 'The Equals'?"

"Oh my God."

"Oh my God, I'm so stupid. And his name is Pat Lloyd. I thought that was Don Henley."

"So did I. By the way, I have no idea what Don Henley looks like."

"Me neither," she said.

"Well, I'm glad I didn't humiliate myself in front of a music legend, that's all I have to say."

"I'm sure at some point you will."

I lay awake in my hotel room later that night listening to Sarah snore and wondering why no one else I knew ever seemed to get themselves into the situations I did. I *was* officially thirty and wondered if there was an age when this kind of behavior should be curbed.

After much deliberation coupled with back-to-back hiccups, I decided to blame the English. They were responsible for my feeling ashamed of my Native American-Jewish-Mormon roots. Had they not subjected me to such blatant discrimination, I would never have tried to use a fake accent in order to blend in with all the other Great Britainers.

I prayed that night. Not only for England, but for my children. I hoped both Earls never had to face the adversity I had seen that night at Dans le Noir. I prayed for their future, for their well-being, and most of all I prayed for them to have manners to send me a thank-you card. I had sent them both a DVD of my half-hour Comedy Central special two months earlier and hadn't heard from either of them since.

CHAPTER SEVEN

Dim Sum and Then Some

Sarah and I had been back from London for almost two months, in which time she had landed herself another man. Lydia, Ivory, and I met Sarah for breakfast and were grilling her about the new guy she had started seeing. "He's really sweet," Sarah informed us.

"He's Hungarian," Ivory said, correcting her. Ivory doesn't often mince her words and has a different way of expressing herself than I do. Her style is more direct and she doesn't lie. While she is a very supportive friend, she makes no bones about telling people the absolute truth no matter what. When, months earlier, I had gotten my eyebrows bleached in hopes of making my hair color look more natural, she said, "You look like an albino, and not one of the fun ones. You need to get your money back and have them fix it. If they can't fix it, you're better off without any at all."

"Who cares if he's Hungarian?" Lydia said, defending Sarah. "What's important is the way he treats her."

"Does he have a big penis?" I asked.

"Not sure," Sarah said.

"What does that mean?" Ivory asked.

"We've only dry humped," Sarah told us.

By the way Ivory reacted to this information, you would have thought Sarah had told her that she had become romantically involved with Flavor Flav.

"Dry humping is disgusting," Ivory declared, throwing her fork down onto the table. "It's for junior high–schoolers. What is the point of a guy lying on top of you fully clothed, and then coming in his pants? What does that even mean?"

"It obviously means that the two people involved are at the beginning of a very meaningful relationship," I answered. "What do you think they did in the seventeenth century when there were layers and layers of petticoats and knickers?" I redirected my attention to Sarah. "I have no problem with the dry hump. I think it can be very magical, especially if you've got one of David Hasselhoff's records playing in the background. What's his name again?" I asked, knowing full well what his name was but wanting Sarah to say it aloud.

"Coolio," Sarah said in the lowest voice possible.

"And he's white," I added.

"That's not so bad," Lydia said unconvincingly. "There are a lot of worse names than Coolio."

"Like what?" Ivory asked. "Rumplestiltskin?

"No, like . . . Eminem."

"Yes," I said, "but Eminem is a rapper. At least he has some tie to the African-American community. Coolio is Hungarian."

"Does Coolio rap?" Ivory asked Sarah.

"I don't think so," she said.

"I think you'd know if he rapped," I told her. "That's not exactly something you just do on the side."

"That can't be his real name," Ivory said.

"It's not," Sarah said. "He told me the other day that it was time for me to start calling him by his first name, but I have no idea what it is. Everyone calls him Coolio."

"I'm sorry, but that is a really ridiculous nickname. That's worse than Sugar Tits," I said, remembering what was written under my high school yearbook picture.

"Chelsea," Lydia jumped in. "I don't think you have any room to make fun of Sarah's fat, smelly boyfriend. You dated Big Red and then got dumped by him."

"This is true," I said. "But Big Red was cute in a . . . different kind of . . . way."

"No he wasn't," all three of them said in unison.

"The point is," Lydia announced, "that you like him and he likes you, and after everything that's happened to you in the past year, you deserve it." Lydia was of course referring to Sarah being broken up with by her fiancé two weeks before their wedding.

"Do you have a thing for foreigners?" Ivory asked Sarah, realizing a pattern.

"I think it's wonderful," Lydia declared.

"Wonderful is a word that should really only be used by gay men," I said to Lydia.

"It really is," Ivory agreed.

"Shut up," Lydia said to both of us. "Just shut up."

Lydia was experimenting with her newfound positivity and it was hard to get used to such a drastic change. A month earlier, after popping two Vicodin on a plane from L.A. to New York, Lydia had cheated on her boyfriend of three years with the Navy SEAL sitting next to her. They were in a full make-out session until the flight attendant approached her and said there had been several complaints from other passengers about "groans" they had heard coming from her aisle. Based on her therapist's advice, Lydia joined the Landmark Forum, one of those life-enhancement seminars, and she already had a completely new lease on life. She had become increasingly sympathetic and supportive, and it was becoming almost intolerable.

"I want a massage," I announced.

"Me too," Sarah said. "I'm dying for one."

"You're not going to get in anywhere on a Saturday," Ivory told us.

I turned and looked at Ivory. "Hey, Debbie Downer, what exactly is your problem today?"

"Sorry," she said. "I had a rough night."

"Why?"

"I went to Air Conditioning." Air Conditioning was a new bar that had opened up down the street from Ivory's apartment. She had been there every night since its opening two weeks earlier.

"With who?" I asked her.

"Myself," she said. "I went by myself."

The three of us looked at her pitifully. "You're a real hot mess," I told her.

"Believe me, I know. You know you're a hot mess when the only person buying you drinks all night is yourself," she told us.

"Isn't Air Conditioning a dance club?" asked Lydia.

"Yes," I said to Lydia, and turned to Ivory. "Who were you dancing with?"

"Myself." Ivory had been unemployed for the past nine months and it had clearly started taking its toll. "You know how you know you're really a hot mess?" she asked us all. "When you make friends with a group of people at a bar, and as you're walking away at the end of the night, you turn around to wave good-bye, and none of them are even looking in your direction."

I turned to Sarah to avoid looking at Ivory any longer. "There's a bunch of those little shitholes on Pico where you can get a massage and you don't need an appointment. You can just walk in. But they're kind of gross," I told Sarah. "To be honest, I really don't care; I need a massage."

"Me too," Sarah said. "Let's go."

We paid our check and jumped in Sarah's car since I was on my moped. After walking into three different places on Pico that had no availability, we found a spot that had a screen door with Japanese writing above it.

Inside, the carpeting was gray with a large dark stain right in front of a tall white counter. Behind the counter there were three Japanese women, all wearing alarmingly bright lipstick. On the wall behind them, an enormous print of a red rose hung with a black Formica frame holding it in place. It was by far the dirtiest place I had ever voluntarily walked into, and that's including a barn I had once passed out in after a pie-eating contest.

"Hi," Sarah said in her sweet, high voice. "Do you have any massages available?"

The three women looked at each other, and then the head Asian said, "Wicense, please."

"I'm sorry?" Sarah asked.

"We need wicense before massage." Sarah looked at me to see if I knew what the woman was saying—since I've been known to have an ear for different dialects.

"License?" I asked.

"Yeah, wicense," she said again.

"Oh my God," Sarah said under her breath, digging through her purse to find her license.

"Why the hell do they need our license?" I asked her. "Are we getting pulled over?"

"Must pay fuhst."

"Before the massage?" I asked the head Asian.

"Yes," she said, smiling. "Before."

"This is ridiculous," Sarah said again.

"I know, but my back is killing me. I need someone to get these knots out."

"This is obviously a whore house," she said under her breath.

I handed the woman my license.

"What are you doing?" Sarah asked me.

"Well, I don't care if it is a whore house, I'm sure they know how to give massages too," I told her. Then I looked back at the head mistress, Dim Sum. "Do you give massages or just happy endings?"

"No happy ending here!" she screamed.

"Oh, Jesus," Sarah groaned.

"You pay fuhst," Dim Sum barked. "One hundred dollah."

"A hundred bucks?"

"You pay fuhst," she said. "Cash only."

"That seems pretty steep for a place that doesn't even go down on us," I mumbled to Sarah as I got money out of my bra.

"You go in back and lay down!" Dim Sum was looking at me, and one of the younger girls standing behind her nodded her head and smiled at me. I looked at Sarah, who was watching Dim Sum put the money I had handed her directly into her pants pocket.

My future masseuse came out from behind the counter and was wearing a white cotton miniskirt that barely covered her ass, which, by the way, was the size of a mini DVD. She had on four-inch white stiletto pumps holding up the two cigarettes she had for legs, and long black hair that left a distinct smell of wonton soup in its wake. I surmised that, without heels, she couldn't have been more than four-feet-eleven inches, which normally I would find adorable, but only if the person is extremely overweight.

She led me down the hall to a room, opened the door, and said, "Go lay down." Inside the room there was a twin bed with white sheets on it and a small chest of drawers next to it made out of the same black Formica as the picture frame in the lobby. Obviously, this was a furniture set Dim Sum had registered for at the Japanese version of Pier One. From the chest of drawers, the girl pulled out three large white towels and placed them down on top of the bed. *See*, I thought to myself. *This isn't so bad. At least they're hygienic.*

Then she closed the door and stood facing me with her arms folded. I wanted her to know that I wasn't some lesbian trying to get some action, I simply wanted a massage. . . . Although, to be perfectly honest, there has been an occasion or two where I've received massages that were so enjoyable and relaxing that had the masseuse buried her head in my hot pocket, I probably wouldn't have put up much of a fight.

I didn't know what my next move should be, so I opted for some light stretching.

"Cwothes off! Underwear stay on!" she said after I had stepped into a deep lunge.

"Okay, okay. Can we at least turn the lights off?" I asked her, not feeling entirely comfortable getting naked in front of someone who I could carry in a Baby Bjorn.

After I received no response from the masseuse I had nicknamed Memoirs of a Geisha, I started to unzip my jeans while hopping on one foot to take off one of my boots. I didn't understand why she had to watch me undress. I wanted to remind her that I wasn't the prostitute in this situation; I was just a nice girl from New Jersey trying to get a back rub.

A normal person would have realized at this point that things were not on the up and up, but I have always been willing to forgo standard operating procedure for an activity that requires you to do nothing in return. "Do you think you'd be more comfortable without those shoes on?" I asked. "They must be killing your feet." I wanted to make this a pleasant experience for us both.

Once I was down to my bra and underwear, I turned my back in modesty to take off my bra, then jumped onto the bed, which had as much bounce as a dining room table.

I put my face directly down on the towel, with no pillow, and put my arms to my sides. "On your mark, get set, go!" I yelled.

"Put this over your tushy," she said, handing me a washcloth large enough to cover one half of an ass cheek. Being on my stomach, and not being able to perfectly place the towel, I spastically put it over the center of the back of my thong in order to cover a little of each cheek.

The first thing I felt was a towel on the back of my shoulder. I wasn't familiar with this kind of technique but felt it was best I kept my mouth shut. For the next ten minutes she continued rubbing my back through the towel, so the primary sensation I was feeling was the towel, which wasn't much different than getting a massage after rolling around in a pile of sand. If anything, this was more of an exfoliation.

I found it ironic, considering my surroundings, that I was the one being cleaned off with a towel, but obviously Memoirs of a Geisha danced to the beat of her own drummer. Or hummer. Whichever. The point is, I was expecting her to make some hand-to-skin contact once she had disinfected me. This never happened. The next twenty minutes were spent in the same manner, with her using a towel to rub me. It became apparent that she hadn't been cleaning me at all. That this was, in fact, the massage.

I wanted to inform her that if this was the way she gave happy endings, it was no wonder they were empty on a Saturday. If there was any service being offered here it was blue balls. . . . Unlike some women, I can sympathize with what blue balls can do to a man because of some early childhood experiences.

I thought back to when I was thirteen and on my very first date with Justin Ledwith. We were in a movie theater in Martha's Vineyard and he had put his arm around me, but even with all my advances, he refused to lean in for some tongue. I put my hand on his knee repeatedly, slowly moving toward his upper thigh, repeatedly brushing by his ball sack, over and over, to no avail. By the end of *Who Framed Roger Rabbit*, I was so hard up for some action, I practically finger-blasted myself.

I craned my neck to look back over my shoulder at Memoirs of a Geisha questioningly, to somehow convey to her that this wasn't something I was enjoying. "You likey?" she asked me.

"No. No likey." I took the towel out of her hand and threw it on the floor. "No towel," I said, and grabbed her hand to redirect it to my back. "Rub my skin."

It was clear she didn't understand what I was saying because she walked out of the room and shut the door. A minute later Dim Sum walked in without Memoirs, but with another heavier Asian who weighed close to three hundred pounds and may have very well been a Sumo wrestler. My instincts told me that it was a woman, but I couldn't be sure.

"You no want massage!" Dim Sum yelled.

"Yes, yes, I do want massage," I told her. "Just not with that softscrub towel."

"You want sucky sucky! No sucky sucky here!"

"Huh?" I asked.

"This not sucky sucky place, we don't do that, wesbian!"

"No," I argued. "I don't want sucky sucky, I just want a massage. It's okay if she doesn't know how to give a massage, but could she at least tickle my back?"

"No happy ending!" she yelled, getting louder.

"I don't want a happy ending, you hot mess, I just want a little back rub. She can even just write letters on my back, if that's easier, and I'll guess what they are. I'm really not trying to be difficult." It was mildly humiliating to be arguing with Dim Sum while I was lying naked on a table and being called a wesbian.

"Listen, I'm not the police, I'm not going to tell anyone about this place. I don't care if there are girls giving handjobs in the next room, right this very minute. I just want a goddamn massage."

"You are bad girl, we have no bad girls here," she said, shaking her head.

That was it."Listen, Dim Sum, you little fuck fuck, I didn't pay a hundred dollars for a fucking towel rub. It hurts!"

"You bad bad girl, you go home, no sucky sucky here!"

"Oh, for fuck's sake, whatever," I said as I got up to get

dressed. Before I could grab any clothing, the Sumo grabbed my shoulders, and forced me back down, this time with my back on the table, and then laid on top of me face-to-face. She was heavy, and reeked of beef with broccoli.

My boobs were being flattened and hadn't been in this much pain since I had hooked up with a thirty-year-old who wore braces. They were the clear kind and I didn't realize he even had them until he undid my bra and headed toward my areola.

My breathing was becoming strained and my eyes were starting to roll back in my head. "No!" I yelled. Mustering up my last ounce of strength, I put my forehead to hers, grabbed her cheeks, and screamed, "My body, my choice!"

Finally, Tons of Fun rolled off me and they both stood there while I got dressed.

"I'd like my hundred dollars back," I told Dim Sum.

"I don't think so, buddy," Dim Sum replied in perfect English.

"Well, I want my license," I told her. She reached in her pocket and held it above her head as she walked out of the room and headed toward the front door. Once she reached the door, she leaned outside and threw my license onto the sidewalk. I looked at both of them, horrified. "This is no way to run a business," I told Dim Sum, and then looked at Tons of Fun. "And you might want to lay off the carbs, you fucking wildebeest."

I walked outside and called Sarah's cell phone. She picked up on the first ring. "Are you still in there?" I asked her.

"No," she said, "are you kidding? I hightailed it. I'm at Whole Foods down the street. I was not about to get a massage there."

"Oh, that's nice, thanks for leaving me."

"I'm right down the street," she said. "Just walk down here. I thought you'd be an hour."

"I got kicked out."

"What?"

"Yeah. They kicked me out and told me never to come back, and called me a wesbian."

"What?"

"Yeah, and that's not the worst of it," I told her. "I think I just got dry humped. By a woman. And paid for it."

CHAPTER EIGHT

Barking up the Wrong Tree

I spent the better part of my early twenties being too much of a weakling to tell my friends that I had absolutely no interest in picking them up from airports, seeing them perform in their improvisation troupes, or, the worst of all three, dog-sitting. I don't have a problem with animals in general, but I'm just not one of those people who's looking to pack my schedule with some extra one-on-one time with a friend's dog.

I also don't appreciate people who celebrate their dog's birthday with "dog parties," and then invite their friends who don't even have dogs. I understand why people like dogs, and I think they definitely bring more to the table than cats or those godforsaken ferrets, but I don't think it's healthy for people to treat their dogs like they are real people. Another thing I take issue with are people who take their dogs on "play dates," or even worse, people who choose to dress their dogs up in outfits better suited for homosexuals participating in a gay pride parade. Dog costumes are right up there with something else I find particularly offensive: sweater vests.

A friend of mine, Lesley, whom I had dog-sat for in the past, called me to tell me she and her sixty-year-old boyfriend were going away for a long weekend to celebrate the holiday. Why they assumed I had no plans of my own for Flag Day was not only insulting on a personal level, but on a national level as well.

"We wanted to know if you wanted to dog-sit for Pepper and Daisy," she said to me over the phone while I was trying to figure out the best way to disguise a huge bruise I had on my upper arm from a Yahtzee tournament I had participated in the night before. I wanted to tell her that I'd rather be forced to watch a *Lord of the Rings* marathon and then be raped by a hobbit than dog-sit for anyone. But I hadn't had enough therapy at that point to know about creating boundaries, so instead I said, "Definitely!"

Lesley and her father/boyfriend live in a big house in Brentwood and are under the impression that anyone who lives in an apartment would jump at the chance to sleep in a real live house. This is not the case, unless of course you were raised in a shelter. Or if the house you're pet-sitting in has a pool, butler, steam room, and a closet filled with cocaine. I take absolutely no pleasure in staying at other people's homes. Even when I go to visit a friend in another city, I rarely stay at their place. I prefer hotels and not having to worry about walking around naked or farting, which happens almost every time I get into a cross-legged position. The biggest discomfort of all is sleeping in someone else's bed, which is not appealing on any level—unless, of course, penetration is involved.

I went by later that day to pick up the keys from Lesley, giving myself the middle finger the whole way there. Not only was it imperative that I sleep at their house because if Pepper, their newest dog, wasn't put in a crate at night she'd shit all over the floor, but they also made it a regular habit to cook fresh ground hamburger meat twice a week for Daisy, their golden retriever. One of my responsibilities would include taking a big log of hamburger meat out of the freezer, defrosting it, and then cooking it in a frying pan. Each batch was meant to last for three days, but with me also snacking on it regularly, I ended up having to make three to four batches.

I had met Lesley a couple of years earlier when I had worked at a restaurant called Chaya Venice. I wasn't even really good friends with her, but I made the mistake of dog-sitting for another girl at work, and word spread like an AMBER Alert. The most ridiculous thing about it was I had never led anyone to believe I even liked dogs that much. The only animals I had ever been publicly effusive about were apes. Aside from their bright pink assholes that stick out like toilet plungers, I think that as far as personalities go, they really have the most to offer.

The minute I arrived at Lesley's house, insanity ensued. Anytime the front door was opened, Lesley had a full-on wrestling match with Daisy, the big dog, while simultaneously shooing away Pepper, the Peekapoo, so that neither would escape.

My feeling is, if a dog is that hard up to break free, let it go. It's like a boyfriend who wants to break up. We all know the old adage, "If you set someone free, and he never comes back, then he was never yours." I understand the main fear with setting dogs loose is that they could get hit by a car, but so could an ex-boyfriend. That's just a chance you have to take.

In between her screaming "Daisy, down!" and "Pepper, no!," we chitchatted and she reminded me how to use all the TVs and DVD players and told me where the dog park was. I wanted to tell her that I'd sooner buy an RV and drive across the country with Lorenzo Lamas than hang out for the afternoon at a smelly park covered in dog shit.

Lesley's lover, Jerry, came out midway through my briefing and reminded me not to leave any small items out, referring to the last time I dog-sat, when Daisy ate my cell phone, contact-lens case, and an entire box of Godiva chocolates I had found in their cupboard. They were nice enough to reimburse me for the phone, but obviously I didn't tell them about the box of chocolates since I was the one who left them out in the first place. The important lesson I learned from that is that dogs do not necessarily go into cardiac arrest if they have chocolate. They also need to have a history of alcoholism, smoking, and/or a drug dependency.

Jerry was a really nice guy, but my main problem with him was that he had a double-decker toe. His middle toe laid directly on top of his index toe. If this is the hand you're dealt in life, then fine, but at least have the courtesy to keep the situation under wraps until all parties have been fully prepped for an unveiling. He constantly walked around in open-toed sandals as if nothing whatsoever was wrong. I find that to be not only arrogant, but Jerry obviously had no concern for other people's comfort levels or gag reflexes, which is just plain disrespectful.

The worst part was that while I was trying not to stare at his deformity, the stupid little dog, Pepper, insisted on jumping up and down—ricocheting off my leg, back onto the floor, and up again—and I had to pretend in front of his owners that he was one of the cutest things I'd ever seen.

The most insulting part of this dog-sitting bonanza is that Lesley insisted on paying me forty dollars a day. I know that's kind of generous, but at the time, I was a regular on a television show, and although it was on a cable vagina network, I was making plenty of money to live on. I was dog-sitting as a favor, not to rake in an extra one hundred and sixty bucks over a four-day period.

I left there wondering why I was constantly getting myself into situations that I wanted no part of. I called my boyfriend at the time, Mohammed. That wasn't his actual name, but he was half Persian, which he failed to inform me of until our third date, and as punishment for trying to cover up his heritage, I thought it best to only refer to him as the most Middle Eastern name I could think of: Mohammed. Being Persian is very similar to the double-decker toe. These are things you need to brace another person for.

Heavy M and I had been dating for a couple of months and we pretty much spent every night together. We clicked instantly, and I had wondered if maybe he was the perfect match for my personality, but also wrestled with the idea of our children being raised by the Ayatollah. If I had to compare him to well-known celebrities, I'd say he looked like a cross between David Duchovny and Will Smith. He looked a lot like David, but his skin had the tone that some people would refer to as olive. The olives I come in contact with the most are green, so I would more accurately describe his skin tone as a café latte. He was definitely sexy due to having the same laid-back personality as Matthew McConaughey, minus having the inclination to play the bongos while high on the Mary Jane.

"Yo, yo, yo," I said as he picked up the phone. "I have some bad news."

"What?"

"I'm dog-sitting for some friends of mine you've never met, and probably never will. They have a house in Brentwood and I have to sleep there for the next three nights."

"Why are you doing that?" he asked.

"Because I'm an asshole."

"Well, why do you have to sleep there?"

"Because their little Peekapoo can't be left alone at night or he cries."

"What's a Peekapoo?" he asked.

"Like a Chihuahua, but worse."

"I hate Chihuahuas."

"I know, she caught me off guard when she called, so I'm just fucked. You can sleep here too," I told him. Mohammed had a beautiful house in the Palisades, so there was definitely no draw for him to be sleeping in a stranger's house down the road.

"Great," he said with the same excitement you'd exude after finding out that Lionel Richie was performing in your hometown. Mohammed was very sarcastic, which is what drew me to him in the first place. He was a real-estate attorney who made his own hours, worked sparsely, and managed to make a fortune, three qualities I am always drawn to in a Persian.

"Do we have to play with them?" he asked.

"Well, no, but it's not like we can hit them," I told him. "I have to take them for walks and stuff, and make sure they're fed, but they're kind of high maintenance, so I totally understand if you don't want to sleep there."

"Uh-huh." He sighed. "Well, I'm going to a rifle range, wanna come?" he asked.

"Why are you going to a rifle range?" I asked him.

"I don't know, I thought it might be interesting to learn how to use a firearm. It might be a good idea for you to learn also, just in case I ever decide to backhand you."

"That's an excellent point, but I think I'm going to go home and pack some stuff for the next few days. And then Fantasia is coming over to clean my apartment, and I have to be there so she doesn't take anything." A month earlier I had come home after my cleaning lady had been there to find my TiVo missing. After refreshing my español via telefonica with a busboy I had kept in touch with since my waitressing days, I mustered up the courage to confront her.

She picked up after three rings and I went for it. "Hola, Fantasia, this is Yelsea."

"Hola, Yelsea!"

"*Donde esta* TiVo?"

Her response was "Okay, bye," and then a dial tone. Fantasia had hung up on me.

The following Monday she brought my TiVo back with major attitude. *"Aqui!"* she yelled as she slammed it down on the table. I didn't understand what her problem was, or why I was then stuck watching twenty-five episodes of *¿Donde Esta Selena*?

The next day I drove over to Lesley's around noon to begin my dog-sitting duties, and the dogs went absolutely nuts the minute I opened the door. You'd think they'd been left alone for an entrire week already.

"Jesus," I moaned as both of them jumped up and down, and Pepper barked in his signature high pitch. "Hi, guys." I feigned enthusiasm as I bent down and pet them both, paranoid that Lesley and Jerry had installed some sort of neighborhood pet-watch video cameras.

I took the dogs outside to the backyard and found a tennis ball on the lawn. The backyard was enclosed by a wall made out of large stones leading up a steep hill so that the dogs couldn't escape.

"All right, guys," I announced, "let's play catch." I threw the ball once and then walked back inside and closed the glass door. I had been there for a total of ten minutes and was already wiped out.

Just as I was falling into a deep sleep on the sofa, I heard loud barking. After fifteen more minutes of this, I creaked my head up and saw a lawnmower at the top of the hill in their backyard with no one operating it. Daisy was nowhere to be found, and Pepper, of course, was doing her usual musical number, which was about as soothing as an Ozzy Osbourne concert.

"Fuck!" I groaned, and jumped up to go outside. I could hear Daisy barking but couldn't see her anywhere.

"Daisy," I called as I tried to catapult myself over the rock base leading to the woods.

"Daisy!" I screamed. "Daisy!"

I looked over into the neighbor's yard and saw Daisy at the base of the tree, barking at a gardener who was hanging above her with his wrists and his feet wrapped around a branch, positioned a foot apart. Like a koala bear.

"Daisy," I hollered as I ran along the side of the incline over to the tree, through thick branches and dirt, and along a side incline that made for very unlevel footing. Why a grown man would be afraid of a golden retriever made about as much sense as Janet Reno casually dating Kanye West.

"Lo siento!" I said. "I'm so sorry! Daisy, get over here!" Daisy turned around and saw me, then ran in the direction of the street at a speed upward of the typical ten miles per hour I've known most dogs to be capable of.

The descent down into the street was a steep one since both homes were set high up on a hill. Boarding a sled and heading downhill on solid pavement would have been less frightening than running down a ninety-degree angle in platforms. Not only did I roll my ankle twice, I fell into a double somersault, which, to my complete shock, turned into a round-off leading into a triple back handspring, ending with me at the bottom of the neighbor's driveway with two bloody knees and a hangnail.

Daisy was at the bottom of the hill running away from me as I was trying to catch her. After a good minute and a half of running in the same exact circle, I realized we were in a holding pattern. I stopped, and so did she.

"Let's go!" I said, and clapped my hands. Then she walked right over to me and sat down. I grabbed her collar and dragged her over to Lesley's driveway and back up the hill. Luckily, I had left the garage door open, and was able to get in through there.

After I brought Pepper in from the back, I went into the bathroom to clean myself up and look for some Band-Aids. Of course, the dogs couldn't be left alone for more than thirty seconds, so instead of using disinfectant or rubbing alchohol, I was treated to the two of them alternately licking the blood off my knees. "Stop it," I yelled, and then before I knew it, I started crying like a baby.

Without collecting my thoughts or gathering any composure, I called Mohammed while simultaneously spitting up.

"Please come over here," I cried, and gave him the address.

Twenty minutes later he was knocking on the front door, which, of course, made both dogs jump up and down like a couple of lunatics. I opened the door feeling incredibly sorry for myself and, once again, burst into tears.

"These dogs are gonna drive me to drink!"

"What happened to your knees?" he asked, noticing I had

a piece of bathroom tissue covering each knee, both soaked in B-positive blood.

"Daisy escaped and I had to run down the hill in my shoes, and it wasn't pretty."

He was very sweet with me, giving me a hug and then taking the dogs into the living room and letting them jump all over him in an effort to allow me some time to comport myself. I went in the bathroom and cleaned myself off, and when I came out, Mohammed was outside throwing the tennis ball with the dogs. He came inside with them when he saw me.

"Are you okay?" he asked.

"I can't understand why I am always falling all over the place," I said, sitting down on the sofa. "You'd think the advantage of having eight years of tap on my side would help me with some of the coordination challenges I seem to regularly find myself up against."

"I take it you're feeling better. Do you think you might cry again?"

"Yes," I said, as the dogs ran over to me, jumping up and down. The big one was at least cute, and as annoying as she was, you couldn't get mad at a golden retriever. The little Peekapoo, on the other hand, wasn't attractive on any level, and that, combined with his high-pitched squeal, made me want to throw him against a wall.

"I feel bad about the feelings I'm having toward this little shit dog," I told Mohammed while simultaneously rubbing Pepper's head. "I don't want to hurt him, but I really feel like if

I have to stay here for three days, I'm going to kill one of them or myself."

"Well, you should definitely not kill one of the dogs," he said. "You could go to prison."

"Thanks."

"That dog is really stupid. I don't understand people's obsession with little dogs," he said. "I'll stay here with you."

"Thank you," I told him, flattered he would be willing to support me in that way. "Is there any chance you would sleep here by yourself?" I asked him.

"No."

What I did remember from last time is that Pepper spent the majority of the night crying in his cage like a little bitch, but I wasn't about to give Mohammed the heads-up on that one.

"They have the DVD box set of all four seasons of *Sex and the City*," I said. "Wanna watch?"

"No."

"What about all five seasons of *Saved by the Bell*?"

"Fine."

We walked into their media room and closed the door, leaving the dogs in the hall to fend for themselves. It was time for a break. As we were watching one of the episodes I turned to Mohammed. "Who would you rather have sex with, Screech or Star Jones?"

"Star Jones now, or before her gastric bypass?"

"Before."

"Who's giving and who's taking?" he asked.

"Screech is giving, and you'd have to go down on Star Jones for one hour . . . after she went jogging."

"I choose both," he said.

"Interesting. Very interesting."

"Wanna have sex in their bed?" he asked.

"Well, yeah, but it's gonna have to be a quickie," I told him. "I need to run some errands."

We walked out of the media room, and of course the moment the dogs heard the door open they were running down the hallway from the living room, drooling all over the place. We went into the bedroom, and I put Pepper in his crate. "Are the sheets clean?" Mohammed asked.

"Yes."

"Then why are they covered in dog hair?" he asked, throwing the comforter on the floor.

"Gross. I really think dogs are unsanitary," I said. "I think it's actually only the comforter. The sheets should be clean."

"They are," he agreed, inspecting them. "What do you think is worse? Allowing them to sleep in the bed with you, or putting them in a cage?"

"Allowing them to sleep in the bed with you. By the way, Daisy sleeps in the bed." Pepper started yapping again and I walked over and let him out of his cage. We jumped into bed and started fooling around. Within seconds, both dogs were on the bed with us.

"This isn't going to work," I said.

"Go get them out of the room and close the door," he suggested.

"Just forget it," I said, losing interest and getting dressed.

"I have to go pick up my dry cleaning anyway. Just take your nap, and we'll go out to dinner. We'd have better luck having sex in your car."

"I'm open to that."

I grabbed my keys and headed to the door as the dogs engaged in the same tug-of-war routine that happened when anyone entered or left the house. Once inside my car, I looked down at my black pants that I had changed into after my downhill slalom only to discover I was completely covered in Daisy's hair. I was starting to feel like a real asshole.

An hour later I came back to the house and walked inside. Surprisingly, Daisy was the only one who accosted me upon opening the front door. I walked into the bedroom and found Mohammed lying in bed, still with his clothes off, watching *Dr. Phil* with Pepper cuddled up next to him.

"This dog can't get enough of me," he said, laughing.

"Why are you letting her in the bed? Those sheets are clean; they're gonna get all smelly."

"It's a he, and apparently he's gay," Mohammed declared, still laughing.

"Oh, really?" I asked him. "When did you start speaking Peekapoo?"

"Right after he licked my huge penis."

"I really hope you're kidding," I said, hanging my dry cleaning in the closet.

"No, actually."

I turned around and walked back into the room. "You let Pepper lick your penis?"

"He just did it. I didn't whip it out. I was lying here watching Dr. Phil, who, by the way, has some anger management issues. Doesn't his wife Robin look like she's been hypnotized? I feel like he goes home and beats her. The guy's an egomaniac, and he's not doing a very good job of covering it up by pretending to be interested in other people's problems."

"Can we get back to you and Pepper, please?"

"I was lying here and *he* jumped up and came right for me. I picked him up and threw him on the floor, but he came back again, and, to be honest, it didn't feel so bad."

There was a long silence while I stared at Mohammed, who for some reason thought this was hilarious and couldn't stop laughing. I didn't find it amusing. . . . Maybe a little, but I wasn't about to let him know that until I found out exactly how far they had gone.

"Are you telling me that you hooked up with a Peekapoo?"

"I wouldn't call it hooking up, but yes, I would say there was a line that was crossed, and I blame Pepper."

"Mohammed, that is disgusting and foul. Did you climax?"

"No!" he said. Now he was laughing so hard he was crying. All the while, Pepper was nuzzling up against his neck in a postcoital embrace.

"If a grown man is going to hook up with a dog, you'd think he'd at least pick a respectable-size one," I said, looking at Daisy, who was lying on the floor hiding her head shamefully. "And can you please get him away from your neck? That is really creeping me out."

"I didn't initiate it, Pepper did. And besides, it was for

two seconds. It's not like he gave me a blow job."

"Well, it sounds like a blow job to me," I told him.

"Well, maybe it 'sounds like a blow job' to you, because that's what you think one is."

"Oh, that is low. That is really low."

"I'm kidding!" he yelled.

"No, you're not. You're not kidding. You're not the first person to mention my lack of enthusiasm for blow jobbing, and I'll be perfectly honest with you, maybe it's not my specialty, but making me feel bad about it sure isn't going to help me blow job better."

"I wouldn't actually call what you do a blow job, Chelsea. It's more of a kiss job."

"Oh, that's just great. What kind of person lets a dog lick his penis? That's bestiality."

"No, Chelsea, bestiality is having sex with an animal." Then Pepper jumped up and ran down to his groin, obviously wanting more. This sent Mohammed into a huge eruption of hysterics.

"You have some serious problems and you should really think about talking to someone. Possibly a vet. And I'm not talking about the ones from Vietnam," I told him.

"It's not like I was walking around swinging my dick in the air, taunting him. It was an accident!"

"How someone lets a dog lick his penis *accidentally* is about as believable as me *accidentally* joining a flag-football team."

"I would believe that. I think you've proven once again

today that your hand-eye coordination is tantamount only to Oksana Baiul and Tiger Woods."

"This isn't funny. I leave for an hour and you hook up with a dog? You obviously can't be trusted," I declared, shrugging my shoulders.

"Well, at least I stopped him when he went around to lick my ass."

"Okay," I said as I walked over, picked Pepper up, and tossed him in his cage. "How many times did he lick it?"

"Three or four."

"Your ass or your penis?"

"My penis three or four; my ass, I stopped him before a full lick. I thought that was going too far."

"And did you do anything to Pepper?"

"Chelsea, please."

"Chelsea, please? Please what? I think these are reasonable questions to ask someone who's been intimate with a canine."

"No! I did NOT DO ANYTHING TO PEPPER . . ." Then, after a significant pause . . . "A little smack on the ass."

"That's lovely." For dramatic effect, I crossed my arms and moved my head in a circular motion like a seagull. "How do you feel about yourself?"

"I feel great," he said, changing the channel. "The problem is, Pepper liked it a lot, and he obviously has feelings for me. It's not going to be easy to wean him." Now Pepper was whining in his crate, staring at Mohammed, beckoning for him to come to his rescue. "It's okay, little buddy, we'll let you out again, once

Chelsea calms herself down," Mohammed told him in some sort of gross Persian baby talk.

"Please stop talking to the dog like that."

"Does it make you jealous?" he asked.

"No, it makes me nauseous."

My cell phone rang and I walked over to my purse to get it, all the while keeping my eyes on Mohammed and Pepper. The big dog was holding her head in both of her paws, still not ready to face the situation.

"Yello?" I answered as I picked up the phone.

"I am a real loser," was the first thing Ivory said.

"Why?" I asked, unmoved, as this was not an uncommon way for her to begin a conversation.

"I just woke up alone in my bed with my pants around my ankles, my vibrator in between my legs, and my glasses on."

"You just woke up?" I asked, looking at the clock. "It's five o'clock!"

"That's not really the point."

"Well, don't feel too bad about yourself," I said, returning to the death stare I was giving Mohammed. "Mohammed hooked up with a dog."

"Chelsea!" he hissed as he tossed a pillow at me.

"What kind of dog?" Ivory asked.

"A Peekapoo."

"Ew."

"Yeah."

"Chelsea, shut up, do not tell your friends that!" he said as he got of bed and started to run after me.

"That's right," I told her, scurrying out of the bedroom. "And he liked it!"

I looked over my shoulder and saw Mohammed's penis swinging in the wind while he was chasing me down the hall, making that the second time in my life since I was seven that I had been chased by a penis.

"That's pretty disgusting. I'm feeling a little better about myself now," was the last thing she said before he grabbed the phone out of my hand, hung it up, and then tackled me to the floor. By this time Daisy had come out of her comatose state and was coming to my aid.

"You better watch your ass," I yelled at him in between breaths. "Here comes another dog!"

Once we both caught our breaths, he urged me not to divulge this information to any of my other friends.

"You made your bed, now you have to get blown by a dog in it," I told him. "I just don't understand why you would do something like that."

"I thought it was funny, and you do too."

"You're mistaken." There was something very unsettling about what had taken place. Even more unsettling than walking in on my father's forty-five-year-old black housekeeper cleaning his kitchen in her underwear, with my mother obliviously knitting on a sofa in the living room and my father watching the cleaning lady through binoculars from another sofa twenty feet away.

"Oh, please, I had a cousin whose wife let her dog go down on her," Mohammed informed me.

"What? What are you talking about?! This isn't something that happens on a regular basis, Mohammed! Not in the United States, anyway. I mean, things like this happen, but mostly with horses, and mostly in the south. And by the way," I added, "people go to prison for it. I understand there was no penetration, and maybe this is big in the Middle East, but I would really appreciate it if you took a shower and got dressed. Somehow, I've developed an appetite."

Ivory called me back an hour later and said she was invited to a party in Malibu. "Bring the doggies; it's outside, and I'd love to see them." The fact that she had any interest in seeing dogs she had never met made me realize she was really desperate for company.

Later that afternoon Mohammed and I grabbed the dogs, put them in his SUV, and drove out to Malibu. The house was big and beautiful, like most houses in Malibu, and belonged to some actor who I'd never heard of before. I spent most of the time inside, talking to Ivory and Lydia, and then I decided I should go find Mohammed.

I found him lying on a chaise lounge by the pool, with Pepper in his arms and Daisy nowhere in sight. "What are you doing?" Judging from his closed eyes and the smile on his face, I had woken him from a wet dream. "Where's Daisy?"

"She's on the beach. I tied her leash to the deck, she's fine. I can't let Pepper go; he just keeps attacking my package," he said through clenched teeth. There were several people around and none of them were talking to Mohammed.

"You look like a molester, sitting out here with that dog in a headlock. Let go of him."

"Fine," he said, releasing his grip. "Watch."

Pepper jumped up, squealed, and then buried his head right between Mohammed's legs.

"See? He won't stop! Everybody's been watching."

"This is ridiculous." I was thoroughly annoyed at this point, and walked back inside. Every time I looked outside, it was the same scenario playing out. Mohammed oohing and aahing with Pepper like they were having an affair behind my back. An hour later I had had enough and went and collected my dog whisperer and the two dogs. "Let's go. I'm hot."

The rest of the weekend was spent with Pepper following Mohammed around the house like cheap perfume. After two full days of being rebuffed, Pepper finally gave up and put himself in a corner. Not only did he refuse to eat, but when Mohammed went anywhere near him, Pepper would shake violently and growl. He was spurned by his lover and his heart was breaking.

Mohammed and I eventually broke up, but not because of Pepper. A couple of weeks later he took me to meet his parents, who lived in San Clemente, about an hour's drive away. His father was nice enough, but his mother was not at all what I had expected. Not only was she extremely unpleasant, but she looked exactly like a man. She had an unreasonable amount of facial hair along with what appeared to be a large mole or herpes sore on the corner of her mouth that was sprouting additional facial hair. She had Nick Lachey's body, a deep voice, very small boobies, and a crew cut. It would have come as no surprise if she had walked into the backyard to compete in a rock-hurling competition after dinner.

I did not like the looks of her and was surprised that Mohammed had made no mention of the fact that he had two dads. Not only did she blow her nose several times during dinner, she barely spoke a word to me, and when she did, it was to ask me to pass her a turkey leg.

"What's the deal with your mom?" I asked him on the way home.

"What do you mean?"

"Well, don't you think she's kind of manly?" I asked him. "Does she lift weights?"

Mohammed hit the roof upon hearing the last sentence and said I was a spoiled brat who was disrespectful and had no sensitivity. I was pretty surprised to see that side of him. He had no sense of humor about it, and was being very defensive and nasty. If we couldn't laugh at his mother's appearance, then what kind of future did we have?

"I just asked you a question," I said, hopping out of the car when he dropped me off without even pulling into the driveway. Without a response, he sped away, leaving me standing in the middle of the street.

A year later I ran into him at a Starbucks. I was at the counter ordering a cappuccino when I saw him through the window, seated outside . . . with a Peekapoo. I walked outside and stood in front of him face to face. "Well, well, well. It looks like you really found what you were looking for, ya sick fuck."

A girl from inside walked up and stood next to us, glaring at me. It was clear she was with him.

"Is this your dog?" I asked her.

"No, it's mine," Mohammed answered.

"I'll bet it is, ya sicko. I'll bet it is."

Then I turned to his new girlfriend and smiled big. "He's so great with dogs. You can leave the two of them alone and you never have to worry about any hanky panky. I mean, unless you're gone for more than an hour."

The look on her face was the perfect revenge. I patted her on the shoulder sympathetically, smiled at Mohammed, and turned on my heels to walk away triumphantly, knowing that I had delivered the perfect innuendo with considerable aplomb.

It became clear as I got in my car that Persians are only really good for two things. Oil and hummus.

CHAPTER NINE

Re-Gift

My friend Lydia and I had been living together in Santa Monica for two years. I was having a hard time learning the lesson of why it's not a good idea to live with friends. Along with not drinking and driving, not having sex on the first date, and always carrying a tampon, this was yet another example of me learning my lessons the hard way.

Lydia has the work ethic of Santa Claus: She prefers to take most of the year off. While my work ethic is not much better, at least I can blame my lack of motivation on the fact that Oprah and Dr. Phil now air back-to-back.

Lydia was working freelance for a publicity firm that allowed her to go in for a couple of hours a day, or every other day. She preferred to "work from home," or what I like to call "work from bed." She got the job from a publicist friend of hers named Aubrey, who was a complete and utter basket case.

At around noon on a Wednesday I got an e-mail from Lydia inviting me to Aubrey's birthday dinner that very night. The e-mail was in the form of an Evite and was sent to Ivory, Ivory's roommate Jen, and me. There was one other person on the list—someone I had never heard of but whose name I didn't like the sound of. The number of invitees for her "thirtieth birthday bonanza" totaled five. And the heading read, "Aubrey wants to be with her closest friends for her birthday tonight. Can't wait to see everyone!" Ivory's roommate Jen had met Aubrey once.

Aubrey is the type of girl who insists on telling unbearably long-winded stories that go absolutely nowhere with no point and no punch line. Not only does she present them as if she's doing a one-woman show on Broadway, she takes painfully long pauses, leaving the listener wondering if the story has ended or if she is just making up details as she goes along. The most ridiculous part is that she tells these tales with the same gusto Richard Simmons would use to gear up for a back handspring. She'll build up momentum tantamount to a downhill slalom, only to reveal after a laborious forty-five minute monologue that Mariah Carey likes to take baths with her dog. In between these painfully long diatribes she somehow also manages to insult the listener.

"Chelsea," she said upon meeting me for the first time, "I have to be honest, normally I don't love dark roots on blondes, but it's weird how they kind of frame your face. You're so angular!"

The backhanded compliments are not nearly as annoying as her stories, or the complete and utter disappointment you experience after getting sucked in to one of these tales expecting a pot of gold, only to get a pile of shit. Ignoring her is the obvious option, but it doesn't work. The problem with this tactic is that if you look away or appear disinterested, she'll simply turn up the volume. She'll speak louder and louder until you are paying attention, and if you try to change the subject, she will interrupt you. The simple act of listening becomes exhausting. "Land the fucking plane!" you want to scream at her.

Another unappealing quality about Aubrey is that she is always telling you the kind of person she is. "I'm a very loyal friend," she'll tell you in the middle of one of her stories, with the emphasis on *I'm*. "I'm one of those people who will give someone the shirt off my back," she'll stand up to say, as if she was a rabbi giving a sermon.

It's been my experience that people who make proclamations about themselves are usually the opposite of what they claim to be. If someone truly is a loyal friend, then they wouldn't need to broadcast it; eventually, people will figure it out. Who talks about themselves like that? I have a lot of good friends and not one of them ever introduced themselves by saying, "I'm a very good friend."

The more time I spent around Aubrey, the more I realized that she was simply born in the wrong decade and would have been better off doing vaudeville in the twenties. I made it very clear to Lydia that she wasn't allowed to bring Aubrey around anymore.

Unfortunately, Lydia is not a good listener.

I promptly responded no to the Evite, wrote something about having diarrhea later that night, and headed back to bed to rub one out with my vibrator. A full minute hadn't gone by before the phone rang, which I ignored. Then my cell phone rang. I looked at the screen and saw Lydia's cell phone number. "This is Chelsea," I said upon answering the phone.

"Chelsea!"

"What?"

"Listen, I don't want to go to this fucking dinner either, but she is really upset about turning thirty and she's not speaking to anyone in her family, and she really needs us there."

"What are you talking about, 'needs us there'? I'm not even friends with her, and I don't appreciate getting seven hours' notice for someone's birthday dinner," I told her. "And by the way, the fact that she's not speaking to anyone in her family is a pretty good indicator that *she* is the problem."

"I know, but she had no plans and I feel terrible. It won't be bad if we all go."

"I have pinkeye."

"No, you do not."

"Yes, I do, my eyes are all red."

"That's because you're hungover."

"Listen, I feel bad for her too, but I can't stomach an entire dinner with her. Those stories are just too boring. Plus, I don't have a present for her, and I'm certainly not buying one."

"Just get her something cheap; it's not like you have anything to do today," Lydia said.

That annoyed me. "Listen, you have no idea what I have

planned for my day," I said as I put my vibrator down. "Where are you anyway? You sound like you're in a washing machine."

"I'm in the bathroom, because I didn't want Aubrey to hear me calling you. She thought you were serious about the diarrhea and I told her you were just kidding."

"I was serious about the diarrhea."

"Chelsea, stop it! You need to do me this favor tonight and come. How many of your stand-up shows have I been to?" This was true. Lydia was pretty loyal and she would come to show after show of mine and laugh riotously after every punch line despite the fact that she'd heard it a million times before, even when the jokes were about her.

"Oh, fine! But if my eyes don't clear up, I may have to wear a patch."

"Good, I hope you do."

"I hate you," I said, and hung up the phone.

I needed a gift. I went into my closet and looked for something I hadn't worn yet, or maybe something I hadn't worn in awhile that looked new. I looked at an old pair of boots and wondered if I could pass them off as vintage. I had never re-gifted before and didn't know what the guidelines were. I decided to call Ivory, who, incidentally, had a job that she went to on a daily basis.

"Can you believe this?" I asked her when she picked up the phone.

"No, actually, I can't. Can Aubrey tell if I've viewed the Evite?"

"Yes," I told her. "And Lydia says we all have to go."

"I know. She's instant messaging me right now, saying you're going."

"Apparently I am."

"Well, maybe it will be fun if we all go," Ivory said.

"No, it won't be fun. Can you get her a gift from us?" I asked.

"Chelsea, I'm at work, I don't have time to go out and get her a gift. I'll probably give her something someone gave me. I barely know the girl," she told me.

"That's what I was thinking too. I have a first-aid kit I've never used."

"I have to go," she said hurriedly and hung up.

I looked around my apartment at all the possible things I could re-gift and was torn between a picture frame that held a picture of me and my sisters, and a candle that had only been lit once. My head bobbed back and forth between the candle and the picture frame, the same way it would if I were watching a tennis match. After what seemed like a long period of time, I finally decided I really liked the picture frame, and I would just cut the top part of the candle wick off. Lydia walked in the door as I was looking for my pocketknife.

"Well, that was a hard day of work you put in. It's almost one p.m., you must be exhausted," I said, rummaging through my fanny pack.

"Ugh, Aubrey is so annoying. She's been crying all day, going on and on about turning thirty; it is so fucking depressing. I had to get out of there."

"I'm giving her that candle," I said, pointing at the candle

I had placed on our coffee table right next to an old newspaper I was planning on wrapping it in.

She walked over to take a closer look at the candle. "It's already been used."

"I'm going to cut the wick off," I told her.

"Then how is she going to light it?"

"Not my problem."

"Chelsea," Lydia said, in the same tone my gynecologist used when I told her I would need a month's supply of morning-after pills. "I'm sure you can find something else. You can't give her that."

"Sure I can," I said as I went over to my computer to check my e-mail, since that is primarily what takes up my day. I love e-mail and much prefer it to the telephone. I had two new e-mail messages. The first was from my brother, who sends me daily greeting cards from a site called gbehh.com. This one had a bunny rabbit holding a piece of paper that read, "You're a fag!" There was a personal message from him underneath that said, "Chelsea, I just finished Melvin's taxes, and according to my calculations, last year our father raked in a grand total of $7,300.62!" My brother Greg is an accountant and is constantly updating me regarding our father's finances and tax evasions. None of my brothers or sisters has any idea how our father supports himself, and my brother Greg thinks it's hilarious.

The second e-mail I opened was from my friend Morgan who lives in San Diego. She e-mailed me a picture of her dog. Alone. Morgan is also the girl who gave Ivory a gold cross for her birthday one year. Contrary to her name, Ivory is the most

Jewish person any of us know. She is constantly using Yiddish phrases, loves food more than anyone I know, and is my only Jewish friend who actually goes to temple.

I understand if people want to e-mail pictures of their babies by themselves, but there is no way I'm going to join Kodak's photo gallery to look at a picture of someone's pet standing by itself in front of Niagara Falls. This is not the first time this has happened to me, and I was actually pleased because I had gathered the materials necessary to respond appropriately. I clicked reply and sent Morgan a picture of my cleaning lady. Standing next to the toilet, alone. I attached a message that read, "Not interested? Me neither."

"I'm not letting you give Aubrey that candle, Chelsea," Lydia said as she put the candle back on the shelf where I found it.

"Well, I've spent the last hour trying to find something and I refuse to spend money on a present. Can't we just buy her dinner?"

"Look in that closet, you have tons of shit in there. I'm sure you can find something," she said, pointing to our hall closet the same way someone would yell "Sit" to a dog.

"I'm giving all that stuff to Fantasia," I told her.

"Who is Fantasia?" Lydia asked me.

"Um, I don't know, maybe the cleaning lady we've had for two years?" I reminded her.

"Her name is Florencia, Chelsea."

I stared at her, wondering if this was true. Florencia did have a familiar ring to it. But I could have sworn Florencia was a name from my past.

"Well, whatever," I said. "She's been calling me Yelsea since she started working here and I go along with it. Every time I call her I have to say, 'Hi, Fantasia, this is Yelsea.'"

I was looking through the closet when I found the present that Ivory bought me for my twenty-sixth birthday. Ivory had gone on and on about this present for months leading up to my birthday. "Chelsea, I can't wait to give you this gift!" she kept telling me over and over again. "I know you so well, this is the perfect Chelsea gift." With all the hype she gave it, you would have thought she had bought me a vibrator that could also make tacos.

After three months of enticing me with the "most amazing gift one person could buy another person," she gave me a board game called Rehab. Not only do I make it a personal rule to never play organized games, if an occasion presents itself where I am forced to play one, I prefer it not to take place on a giant piece of paper. It's called a board game because it's supposed to be on a board. This game came with a giant piece of paper the consistency of loose-leaf that had different rehabilitation facilities spread over it, much in the same vein as Monopoly. It came with some wooden pieces that I actually burned one night when we ran out of firewood.

"I've got it!" I yelled to Lydia as I pulled out the Rehab game. Next, I opened up the Yahtzee box that was on top of the closet, stole three of the dice, and put them in the little plastic Rehab bags, along with a couple of the wooden pieces that were partially scorched.

Lydia walked over to the closet. "Oh my God, I forgot about that game. I actually played that one night."

"You did?" I asked. "With who?"

"I don't know. I can't remember."

"Were you alone?"

"I may have been," she said as she opened the refrigerator and took out a bottle of Chardonnay.

Luckily, the box the game came in looked like it could have been new. I wrapped it up in the newspaper I had set aside. Then I took a black Sharpie marker and wrote "To: Aubrey, From: Chelsea" directly on top of the newspaper.

"Wait, Chelsea." Lydia laughed. "Ivory is coming tonight! She'll see the game and realize what you did."

"Oh, who cares?" I exclaimed, exhausted from the day's shenanigans. I needed to burn off some steam. I walked into my bedroom and dropped to do a set of push-ups. After the third, I got up and walked back into the kitchen, where Lydia was sorting through our bills with a confused look on her face. She did this every month, questioning one bill after another, wondering aloud why we would be charged for electricity two consecutive months in a row.

"That's usually how things work, Lydia."

"No, it doesn't make any sense. Last month we were charged $47.32, and this month we were charged $75.45."

I then inspected the bill and explained to her that we never paid last month's bill, and that was the reason for the increase.

"Still, it doesn't make any sense," she said, confused.

"It makes perfect sense," I told her. "If someone's pulling the wool over our eyes, I'm pretty sure it's not Southern California Edison. This isn't Erin Brockovich, Lydia. We're talking about tens of dollars."

Lydia is five years older than me and never has any money. In the entire time I lived with her, she never paid her rent on time. She's the type of person who says, "I'm really broke right now," and then takes off to Vegas for the weekend.

"Well, I'm really broke right now, so I hope this dinner isn't expensive," she said.

"Yeah, so do the rest of us, Lydia. No one wants to go. And why would anyone want to have a birthday dinner with a bunch of friends who are complaining about going? It's sad, is what it is."

"Chelsea, she has no friends."

"Another red flag," I reminded her.

"Okay," she said, lighting a cigarette. "That's it, you're right. Let's have a better attitude."

"Uh-huh," I said, looking at her sideways. "I'm going for a run."

"Fine, but dinner's at seven-thirty," she said as she poured herself a glass of the cheap wine she had opened.

"I think I'll be able to make it back in the next six hours," I said, looking at my watch.

"It's only one thirty?"

"Yes, what time did you think it was?"

She put her glass of wine in the fridge along with the newly opened bottle. "I can't have a drink at one-thirty."

Lydia was a complete mess. The older she got, the more of a disaster she became.

When I got back from my run, Lydia was on the phone with our telephone company asking why we were being charged for a fax line if we hadn't actually received any faxes that month. Along with her electric company conspiracy, she was also under the impression that we were living at Kinkos and faxes should be free.

I grabbed a bottle of water and headed to the shower. After watching *Oprah* and *Dr. Phil*, it was time to do something productive. I had been seeing a therapist for nearly three weeks and was getting the sinking feeling that she was no closer to prescribing me medication than when we first met.

When I told her that Vicodin was to me what cocaine and horse tranquilizers were to Amy Winehouse, and that without it I would not be able to continue performing at such a high level, she tried to explain to me that Vicodin was a pain medication and it wasn't for the depression I was claiming to suffer from.

Not to be outdone, I gently but firmly explained to her that the depression I was suffering from was causing a very large pain in my *head*. It was back and forth with this woman, and I was exhausted. It didn't take me long to realize this was money that could be better spent. I grabbed the yellow pages, skipped right past the list of psychiatrists, and started jotting down names of psychics.

At around 6 p.m., Lydia came into my room to say that Jen and Ivory would be meeting us there. "Great!" I exclaimed.

"I'm looking forward to it! . . . Where is this dinner, again?" I asked her.

"Cobras and Matadors, on Beverly."

"Do they have a full bar?" I asked sternly. I vaguely remembered that Cobras and Matadors only served beer and wine and I am strongly opposed to such limitations. I prefer vodka and I generally like it in mass quantities.

She scrunched up her face. "Sorry."

I shook my head, brushed by her quickly, and walked into the kitchen. I took my flask out of the cupboard and my Ketel One out of the freezer. Now I would not only have to bring my own lemon juice that I routinely carry with me everywhere to mix with my vodka, but I would also have to supply my own vodka. In addition to being at someone's birthday party whose last name I didn't even know, I would also be bartending.

"Do you think they'll have ice?" I asked Lydia. "Or should we empty a couple of ice trays into a beach cooler?"

"I have to stop by the Gap and get her a present," Lydia informed me. "They have that sale rack, so I'm sure I can find something cheap."

We stopped on our way to the restaurant and I waited in the car while Lydia shopped for a total of seven minutes. She came back with two tank tops and a box.

"How much were those?" I asked, wondering how I would feel if I got two tank tops as a thirtieth birthday present.

"Two ninety-nine each."

"That was nice," I said.

We walked into Cobras & Matadors and were led to a

rectangular table. We were the first ones there, so Lydia sat in the seat directly across from me.

The next person to arrive was her friend I had never heard of. Her name was Six. Like the number. I could tell by her outfit that this girl was going to be trouble. She was wearing a plaid miniskirt with black tights and open-toed, high-heeled, red patent-leather sandals. Her present was in a red gift bag tied together with a black ribbon. These were obviously her theme colors.

"Are these the gifts?" she asked as I finally looked up from her shoes. She was pointing at the present that I had placed in the middle of the table with an unsure look on her face. Her hair was black and in a ponytail that was placed about two inches away from her forehead. Her shirt had nothing to do with the rest of her outfit. It was a pink button-down sweater that belonged on Katie Couric.

Her lipstick was whore red, and outlined with black lip liner, or what could have very well been eyeliner. She didn't have a stitch of makeup anywhere else on her face and she was wearing black hoop earrings that must have been made out of limestone, because her lobes looked like they were going to detach from the rest of her ear at any moment. In addition to this, she was blowing bubbles with what I could only assume was a giant gumball.

It was obvious that Lydia and I would need to avoid making eye contact with each other for the rest of the evening. Lydia and I have the maturity level of ten-year-old boys when we drink, and Six's arrival combined with the gifts we were about to give Aubrey was a surefire sign we were bound for one of our laughing fits that usually only results in two things: us looking like complete assholes, or me having to change my underwear.

"So how do you know Aubrey?" I asked Six, trying not to stare at the whale's spout on top of her head.

"We actually just met a couple of days ago," Six told me.

"Oh, how unusual," I said, glaring in Lydia's direction. "And where did you two meet?"

"It was the funniest thing," she told me. "We were both in Trader Joe's looking for a good multivitamin. Can you imagine?"

It was time for a drink. I leaned into my purse and got out my supplies. "Would you like a cocktail?" I asked Six. "They only serve beer and wine here."

"Oh, um, no, that's okay, I'll probably just have some wine, but thank you. Last time I had vodka, I got sick."

"Last time Lydia had vodka, she had sex," I said, referring to the previous weekend, when Lydia hooked up with a stranger. She woke up in the morning and scrambled out of bed to find out what part of town she was in, only to discover that the guy she hooked up with lived in our building.

Aubrey walked in next, and Jen and Ivory were soon to follow. I got up to give Aubrey a hug, but only after Lydia kicked me under the table. There were three seats on each side of the table. Ivory and Jen were waiting to see which seat Aubrey was going to take. "I want to be in the middle, it's *my* birthday," she announced as she moved to sit down next to Lydia and motioned for Ivory to sit down on her other side. Jen took the seat next to Six directly across from Ivory. "This is Six," I said to Jen and Ivory. "She and Aubrey met last week at Trader Joe's."

Ivory looked over at Six, looked at me, opened her menu, and then held it up to cover her face. Ivory was more mature than Lydia and me. She would never laugh directly in front of someone's face; she would wait until they left the room. She also would never judge someone based on their car, job, or drug habit. She is very open-minded and embraces all different cultures. For example, she is close friends with a gray-haired, black drug dealer named Roger, who she will stay up with for entire weekends straight, wandering from one crack-house to another watching him snort cocaine. It doesn't seem to bother her that Roger is in his fifties or that he carries a revolver.

Jen's a little more laid-back than Ivory, Lydia, or me. She's always around, but usually isn't the one who makes a scene. She's had the same job for five years as a manager of an art gallery and has never had a serious boyfriend, nor does she have the interest. She's quite self-sufficient and a little more dignified than the rest of us, except for the one time Ivory and I couldn't find her at a party, only to discover her on our way out of the parking garage, having sex in a station wagon.

The waitress came over to take our drink orders and tell us about the specials. "It's my birthday," Aubrey declared as she stood up and motioned for everyone else to stay seated. Aubrey has a twang not unlike Drew Barrymore when she speaks, but much more condescending. Although she looks nothing like Drew Barrymore, people tell her all the time that she reminds them of Drew Barrymore and she always acts appalled, knowing full well she loves any comparison to a celebrity.

"I want everyone to know that dinner is on me tonight, because I'm about to come into an *inheritance*. I'm paying for everyone."

"Absolutely not," Six chimed in. "Not one of us here is going to let you pay for your own birthday dinner. It's simply unheard of!"

"Yeah," I said under my breath, as I poured some more vodka into my glass under the table.

"Don't be ridiculous, Aubrey," Ivory jumped in. "It's your birthday."

"You're right," she said as she sat back down. "This whole *inheritance* thing is really turning into a drag. I mean, you'd think an *inheritance* would be something to celebrate . . ." She obviously wanted someone to ask about her inheritance, and that someone was going to be me.

"Tell us everything; what is it? *What* is going on?" I said with complete zeal.

"Well," she started, "my parents are millionaires,"—the first of many loud coughs from Lydia was heard at this point—"and as you all know, my brothers and sisters have been fighting over the estate for years." This was the first I had ever heard of this and knew there was no way Ivory or Jen had heard any of this either. I also knew that there was no way her parents were millionaires, because anyone whose parents are millionaires doesn't go around advertising it. I was zooming in on each of my friends with a hard glare, but none of the girls would look in my direction.

"I'm sorry," I interrupted. "Your parents are still alive, right?"

"Yes, they are, but it's all very com-pli-cated," she said slowly, as if the whole concept of an estate would be way too much overload for a brain as small as mine.

"But if they're still alive, can't they decide which children get what?" I asked.

"Yeah," said Ivory matter-of-factly. "You shouldn't be arguing about this with your brothers or sisters." Then she tried to change the subject. "Do you girls all want to split stuff for dinner?"

"Yes!" Lydia jumped in. I was enjoying this and I wanted to hear more. I wanted to know if Aubrey suffered from full-blown hallucinations or if she consciously made these tall tales up in order to get attention. I've been known to lie compulsively too, but only when I'm so intoxicated that I have trouble remembering the difference between fact and fiction.

"My brothers and sisters are all really jealous of me because my parents have left me the most out of everyone," she said, loudly enough to quell Jen and Ivory, who were discussing the menu. She upped the volume another couple of decibels and said, "My brothers and sisters think I don't need the money because of my *screenplay*, but the fact of the matter is (long, dramatic pause) . . . I probably won't see that money for months."

I couldn't wait to see who was going to bite the bullet and ask her about that one. Everyone except for Six pretended like they were looking at their menus. Ivory is very good at tuning things out and was doing just that. Lydia was coughing into her lap, and I was smiling so hard my cheeks started to shake.

"I know, I know, it's all so dramatic," Aubrey said with a wave of her hand in response to no one.

"I can't believe you wrote a screenplay," Six exclaimed. "I'm an actress!"

"Really?" I asked. "Do you have, like, a monologue or anything we could see?" Ivory works in television. Ivory pretended not to hear me and continued looking at the menu. "Ivory," I said loudly, "Six is an actress."

"Anyway!" Aubrey was now screaming, for fear the topic of conversation would move on to someone else. "It's the difference between like three million and ten million dollars, so I want to make sure I get my fair share!"

"Let's open presents!" Ivory exclaimed.

"Okay, okay, okay," Aubrey responded grudgingly, as if we had been begging her to open presents for the past three hours.

The waitress walked over and we all ordered. "Let's not forget a piece of cake at the end for the birthday girl," I told her. Ivory looked in my direction with an unsettlingly calm gaze on her face. "Open mine first," she said to Aubrey, still staring at me pointedly while handing Aubrey a small box.

"Seriously, you guys, you did not have to get me anything."

"Oh, bollocks!" Six interjected.

"I'm sorry, are you British?" Ivory asked her.

"No, but I just got back from England and I love, love, loved it!"

Aubrey finished unwrapping Ivory's present to discover the very same cross that Ivory had gotten from our friend Morgan months earlier.

"Oh my God, this is beautiful! I absolutely love it," Aubrey said as she leaned forward so that Ivory could help her clasp it in the back. Ivory looked at me with a huge smile on her face, and Jen was wiping her mouth with a napkin—before we had been served any food.

Lydia was slurping down her third glass of wine and was too preoccupied with Six's ponytail to realize what was happening. It was amusing to me that Ivory thought she had pulled one over on Aubrey and that we were all pawns in her little game of re-gifting. Little did she know who would be getting the last laugh tonight.

Six took her present off the pile next. Aubrey opened it to find a basket of lotion and bath oils. Lotion and bath oils are the most impersonal gift you can buy someone, which is why it's perfect that when she opened Jen's present next, it was another basket of lotion and bath oils. This was getting good. "Oh, how funny!" Six exclaimed, clapping her hands together.

She reached for my present, but I knew patience was a virtue and that soon I was going to have my moment in the sun. "Open Lydia's first," I told Aubrey as I watched Ivory continue to ride her wave.

"What are you laughing at?" Aubrey asked Lydia, who was

now starting to laugh more and more uncontrollably. This was all too much for her. When Lydia laughs hysterically, it's infectious. It is also not long before she starts snorting. I was trying to avoid losing it completely and kept averting my eyes from Lydia to Ivory, who had assumed Lydia was still laughing at Ivory's clever gift to Aubrey. Ivory was looking at me proudly, like she had given us all a night to remember.

"Let's take a picture!" shouted Aubrey, as she pulled out her camera.

I took this opportunity to walk over behind Ivory's chair and whisper, "You are hilarious, so funny!" and then leaned in, put one arm around Ivory and the other around Aubrey, and smiled like I had just gotten a B12 shot.

I sat back down on my side of the table and Aubrey opened Lydia's gift from the Gap.

"That's sweet," Aubrey said condescendingly to Lydia. "I know you're on a budget."

This was the only time of the night Lydia stopped laughing. I could see her mind scrambling to say something, but surprisingly, she was able to stop herself. The last present was mine. Ivory leaned in with Aubrey, who was squinting to read my writing on the gift.

"Oh, how dear," Aubrey said with a grimace on her face. "I haven't seen newspaper wrapping since the sixties."

"How do you know about the sixties if you're only turning thirty?" I asked her inquisitively.

"Ha, ha, ha, somebody is paying attention," she said with a wink in my direction.

Did this mean she was lying about her age? Aubrey was exactly the type of person who would lie about her age.

She was unwrapping my gift with her head cocked to the side when Ivory's head also cocked to the side. It brought back memories of the synchronized swimming team I had never been part of.

Aubrey pulled the Rehab game out and held it up. Ivory was still unsure of what was taking place and looking at the game the same way you would look at someone you met ten years ago.

"Wait a second! That's the same game I bought you for your birthday," she said, perfectly oblivious.

"Yes," I said, with my teeth closed and eyes wide. "The exact same."

"But where did you get it?" she asked, genuinely perplexed. "I found it at some store in the Valley."

My expression remained the same as I responded, "In my apartment!"

Aubrey was too horrified by her gift to be paying attention to all the commotion at the table. Lydia's composure had long since vanished and she was now vacillating between snorting and violently shaking. Jen has a quieter laugh but had her head in her hands with her shoulders bouncing up and down. I had my drink in between my legs and was trying to redirect the urine that was seeping its way out of my vagina. Six had no idea what was going on, and it was taking Ivory even longer to connect the dots.

"Did somebody already play this?" Aubrey asked as she emptied the mismatched pieces in their little plastic bags that were no longer sealed. That's when Ivory's mouth opened.

I tasted blood in my mouth from biting my lip so hard, but had to retain composure. *What if blood just starts spilling out of my mouth?* I thought. I thought of the scene in *Million Dollar Baby* where Hilary Swank chews up her own tongue trying to kill herself and envisioned Clint Eastwood coming over to my table and telling me I was his "Baklava" or whatever the hell he called her in that movie.

"What is so funny?" Aubrey asked, looking at Lydia, who was face-to-face with the wall next to her, slapping her hands against it.

Any normal person at this point would be completely disgusted by our behavior. Not Aubrey. She was so wrapped up in her own bubble of delusion that the next thing out of her mouth after seeing each one of us laughing hysterically was, "Who wants to make a toast?" Before anyone responded, Aubrey interrupted herself and stood up.

"I just want to say (long, dramatic pause) . . . that without any blood relatives at the table, I want everyone here to know that this has been the single most meaningful birthday of my life. I am the type of person that will remember this for the rest of my life (another long, dramatic pause, this time with tears) . . . I want you to know that when I get my *inheritance*, and my family, who have caused me nothing but pain . . ."

"We're your family now," Ivory interrupted, and got up to give Aubrey a hug.

I stood up. "Oh, Chelsea, that's sweet, you want to go next?" Aubrey asked.

"No, I just need to use the bathroom." I grabbed my things and went to the bathroom. After I was done, I headed straight out the back door, around the front of the restaurant, got in my car, and drove home.

The next morning around 9 a.m. I was checking my e-mail when Lydia walked through the door looking haggard. "Thanks a lot for leaving last night, asshole. I had to sleep over at Aubrey's house with that girl Six. Aubrey ended up crying all night long and telling us it wasn't even her birthday. And then she tried to get us all to take a bath together."

"What?"

"Yeah, Ivory and Jen were so pissed. They both got up and made toasts. Then three hours later we ended up at Formosa, where she reveals that she's actually thirty-six and has no brothers and sisters. They both said they were going to the bathroom and left me there. Ivory took the game back. She said she'd rather give it away to an orphan."

"I can't believe that, what a lunatic!" I said.

"I know. Can you imagine lying about having brothers and sisters? She's a sociopath who—"

"No," I interrupted. "I can't believe Ivory thinks Rehab is an appropriate game for an orphan."

"I'm going to bed," she said, and walked into her room.

I sat at my computer, elated. It turned out that there was someone out there who was even more mentally unstable than me. And that special someone's name was Aubrey.

CHAPTER TEN

Jumped

It was a Friday morning and I was on MySpace exchanging messages with a guy who had asked me to go to dinner. My immediate response was, "How big is your penis?" His return message was, "I've never had any formal complaints."

This made me laugh out loud. As if when women encounter a small penis, we wake up first thing the next morning and lodge a formal grievance with the LAPD. I consider myself to be a very obnoxious person, but even *I* would never tell a guy that he has a small penis.

Men don't seem to understand that, under no circumstances, will we confront them on this issue. That would be on par with telling a girl she has a smelly vagina, which, by the way, is something I have once been told by a woman, but only during a particularly disturbing massage. Most men would never tell a girl her Pikachu smells like a crab cake. It's just not done. But they would have no qualms telling their guy friends. Similarly, if you're a guy and you pull your pants down, and the girl you're with immediately starts text messaging her friends, you have a small penis.

After I decided to never meet this person in public, I looked down at my gut. My body had really taken a turn for the worse, and the surprise party I was throwing for my thirtieth birthday was three weeks away. I knew I wasn't out-and-out fat, and I don't think anyone would have described me as a heifer, but there was definitely some toning up needed. It had gotten to the point that the only body parts I felt comfortable exposing in public were my forearms.

Everything else seemed to be in some state of disrepair, especially my abdomen, which somehow managed to divide itself into three sections when I was sitting cross-legged. Something had to be done, so I closed MySpace and Googled the word "fatass."

While looking at a website for liposuction, I learned that it was a six- to eight-week recovery period, the clincher being that, during that time, I would under no circumstances be able to use street drugs. Obviously I had to think of a more realistic approach.

I decided to call a nutritionist my friend Lydia had used, and set up an appointment for Monday. He asked me to keep a food journal of everything I ate over the weekend. I decided once and for all to commit to eating healthy. I have always worked out, but my diet has never been the best, and I knew things were only going to go downhill after thirty. This was my chance to make a change, and I made a commitment to be completely honest about what I was eating. Unfortunately, that Sunday I had to go to a good friend's baby shower, where there was an abundance of unhealthy food. When I met with Matt, the nutritionist, on Monday morning, I handed him the following list:

FRIDAY

Breakfast	scrambled egg whites with spinach and jack cheese
Lunch	chicken Caesar salad
Dinner	2 crab enchiladas and 2 margaritas

SATURDAY

Breakfast	Zone bar
Lunch	turkey sandwich with cheddar and mayo
Dinner	filet mignon with mashed potatoes, 3 Ketel One and cranberries

SUNDAY

Friend's baby shower

17 jalapeño poppers

1 brick of cheddar cheese/12 whole wheat crackers

14 chicken wings/no bleu cheese dressing

1 bagel with low-fat cream cheese

34 strawberries

8 Bloody Marys

14 pigs in blankets

I thought I had made some healthy choices on Friday and Saturday. Obviously Sunday was a complete disaster, but I'd be lying if I didn't admit to being a little proud of the will power I demonstrated when opting for the whole-wheat crackers to go with my brick of cheddar cheese.

I must have repeated that I had been at my friend's baby shower seven times, and the phrase "I don't normally eat like that" at least four times. I could tell the nutritionist was repulsed, but I explained to him emphatically that I was ready to commit to being a healthy eater, and that jalapeño poppers were a thing of the past. "I wanted to go out with a bang," I told him, staring at my stomach with my head hanging down.

He explained to me what clean eating was and had a whole diagram with charts, percentages, a pointer, and a blackboard. The whole presentation was no different than what you'd see on an episode of *CSI: Miami*.

Then Mark weighed me and measured my body fat with a body-fat clipper. I was 131 pounds and 25.2 percent body fat. "Is that good?" I asked him.

"No."

Mark was about six-two with blond hair on his head, but no hair anywhere else. Not my favorite quality in a man, but I guess when you get down to 1 percent body fat, you're also required to wax yourself.

We talked for an hour about what I had to do to get lean, and he put together a meal and exercise program for me and showed me how to log on to a website where I would type in every morsel of food that entered my body. I would also have to change up my exercise routine. He explained that since I had been jogging for so many years, I'd plateaued. He suggested that any martial arts or kickboxing would be just the kind of jump start my body needed.

I explained to Mark that I had been kicked out of three separate aerobics classes due to severe motor challenges when moving my arms and legs in different directions.

He seemed suspicious of me and I didn't want him to think I was making up excuses. I told him about the first time I took a step class, when I hit my neighbor after I had somehow managed in my confusion to step my way over to her step. The first time I backhanded her, the instructor let it slide. The second time, my victim had fallen to the floor and was covering one side of her face when the music came to a screeching halt. I would have been an idiot not to figure out that I had made a major step faux pas.

The last incident was during a class called the Bar Method, which uses ballet bars and poses that focus on concentrated areas. This was the only class I hadn't been kicked out of due to my spastic hand-eye coordination. But I did get kicked out for giving the instructor the finger.

Mark recommended I try boxing.

"Done," I told him. "What's next?"

He then guided me through all my dietary options, like how to replace a yam with four ounces of broccoli if I so desired. "Let's talk alcohol. Are you with me?" I asked as I pounded one fist on his table.

"No. Alcohol is all sugar," he replied. I tried to remain calm.

"Okay," I said, taking a deep breath. "What about vodka?"

"Nope."

"I'm not following you."

"Vodka is empty calories, Chelsea. Alcohol is carbs that cannot be used for energy."

"Well, that's not true," I told him. "I get tons of energy when I drink."

"Vodka turns to sugar, Chelsea, and whatever you're mixing it with is going to have a lot of sugar."

"Well, isn't there anything that doesn't have sugar that I can mix it with?"

"You can drink it straight, or use fresh lemon juice."

"I can do that."

"Chelsea, alcohol slows down your metabolism and is not going to help you get lean. You can have one drink a week, but any more than that is going to bloat you."

I was left with no choice but to cover my ears and shake my head from side to side. It's not easy to hear negative stuff about the person closest to you, even if it is true. He had obviously never seen an episode of *Jerry Springer*.

"Listen up, Mark. I am committed to this, but I absolutely must drink more than once a week."

"How many do you need?"

"Well, I'm a comedian."

"How many do you need?"

I tried to undershoot in order to sound like I didn't have a problem. "How about seven?"

"A week?"

"Yes."

"No," he responded. "You can have two drinks a week. Vodka with lemon juice and that is it."

I was silent. My eyes watered and I looked away to avoid Mark's gaze. I didn't want him to see me get emotional this early in our relationship, but the things he was saying were hurtful, and there was no denying that.

I decided on the way home from my visit with Mark that I would just not allow myself to drink as much as I'd like. Something had to be done about my body, and it needed to be done in time for my thirtieth birthday.

I drove straight to a kickboxing gym around the corner from my house and bought fifteen classes on the spot. I explained to the woman at the front desk that I could only focus on one body region at a time. I could box or I could kick, but I would not be able to do both at the same time. She suggested I take private lessons with a trainer until I felt ready to join a group class.

"Would that mean that I wouldn't have to clap at the end of the class?" I asked her. "Because I would really like to avoid that."

"You don't have to do that," she informed me.

"Great, let's get this party started," I told her as I triumphantly kicked out one leg and knocked over the table next to me. "Sorry."

I met my personal trainer, Brad, and he was very patient with me. He told me he would incorporate the kicking part only when he felt I was ready. He understood my desire not to be humiliated in front of an entire class again. Surprisingly, boxing turned out to be fun, and something I could actually do.

Three weeks and six drinks later, I went for my third weigh-in. I had lost 4 percent body fat and three pounds. I felt amazing, had more energy than I'd ever had in my life, and was now a believer that muscle does indeed take up less space than fat. I didn't care about only losing three pounds because I could see a major difference in my body. I noticed little muscle lines down the side of my stomach starting to form a two-pack.

This diet was actually working. No diet had ever worked for me in my life. I was the only one of my friends who had tried the Atkins diet and gained four pounds. Not to mention that after being on it for a week straight, my apartment, car, and all of my clothes smelled like a cheeseburger. Up until I met Mark, I was convinced I was having the same life experience with food that Paula Abdul was having with her meds. We were both hanging on by a thread.

I was practically skipping out the door of Mark's office after I jumped into his arms and wrapped my legs around him, elated. "I love you!" I screamed. I knew I still had a little way to go before I'd be where I wanted, but I was just thrilled to know that I had stuck to a program that was actually working.

My boxing classes with Brad were amazing. He told me that I had a lot of resentment inside, and this was a great way to get in shape and also take out all of the anger I had stored about Pearl Harbor.

I would leave class so pumped up that I'd walk onto the street almost hoping to get mugged. I knew I could kick some serious ass and had dreams of heading downtown to an unsafe neighborhood just to test out my mad skillz.

Once in my car after class, I called my sister, my mother, and Lydia to tell them the great news. After not one of those people answered their phone, I decided I would celebrate with a coffee from Starbucks. This was definitely a "new me." Just weeks earlier, if I had cause to celebrate, I would have headed straight to the nearest California Pizza Kitchen and ordered two spinach and artichoke dips back-to-back.

I walked in, decided to treat myself to a Frappuccino instead of my standard nonfat cappuccino, and then, before I knew it, I also ordered a turkey pesto sandwich, a coffee cake, a rocky-road brownie, one raspberry arugula salad, a fruit-and-cheese plate, three chocolate-covered graham crackers, and a chocolate-chip muffin. "Fuck it," I said to the Samoan woman working the counter. "I'm going to town."

I gathered up all of my purchases and bounced right out to my car to head home. I got a picnic blanket out of my closet that I had inherited from my former roommate Cameltoe, spread it on the bed and put on the lobster bib that came with it, and then got under the covers, turned on Lifetime, and dove headfirst into my rocky-road brownie. After shoveling all my perishables down my trachea, and on the heels of my third chocolate-covered graham cracker, I decided I wanted to vacuum, which was disappointing since my apartment is covered in Spanish tile. Then I thought about masturbating, but remembered my vibrator was in the shop. I had a ridiculous amount of energy and needed an outlet for it. I had to do something. I couldn't sit in bed, so I got up, went into the kitchen, and got out my mop.

My mother had actually purchased the mop for me years before, and it hadn't been used since. I couldn't think of a better time to get involved with my apartment's personal hygiene. After I filled up a salad bowl with water and shampoo, I moved all of the furniture in my living room and kitchen against the wall so that I could really get at the floor.

After thirty minutes of full-blown mania, I decided to rearrange my furniture. I hadn't had this much energy since splitting an eight ball with my rabbi at my bat mitzvah. I put in another good nine-and-a-half minutes of elbow grease before I lost any and all interest in finishing what I had started. I couldn't imagine what my cleaning lady, Fantasia, had to hop herself up on to get through a solid eight hours of this shit. It occurred to me that it probably came easier to Mexicans, considering that they inherit the cleaning gene, but I still had a huge amount of respect for her.

All of a sudden I felt extremely wiped out. I walked back into my room, got under my covers, pulled on my eyeshades, and passed out. Two-and-a-half hours later, my phone rang. I had woken up from a dream where I was still in high school and thought it was the bell. I looked around my room in complete confusion, wondering who I had hooked up with in order to end up here. I didn't understand why the bell kept ringing until I looked over and saw my cell phone on my nightstand. Right next to the wrapper of my turkey pesto sandwich.

I answered the phone and it was Lydia. Apparently, I had agreed to pick her up from the airport and I was an hour late. No wonder she hadn't answered her phone earlier. I felt like I'd been in some sort of nuclear explosion. My head was pounding. I had left my contacts in and they were having trouble finding their way back to the centers of my eyes. I felt exactly the way people describe feeling after being slipped a roofie, minus the anal pain. It occurred to me that what I may have been suffering from was a sugar hangover. I hadn't really had any chocolate in weeks, and my body was completely appalled with what I had shoved into it.

I slowly got out of bed and held onto my desk, and then the wall, as I tried to maintain my footing on the way into the bathroom. I looked in the mirror to see my hair matted to my forehead and some chocolate stuck to the side of one of my cheeks. "When did I get bangs?" I wondered out loud. What a disaster. I walked out of the bedroom and slammed my shin straight into a leg of the couch that was now sitting in my kitchen. "Fuck me!" I screamed as I hopped up and down on one foot and then fell over. I craned my neck to look around the corner at the clock in my kitchen, which read 3:59 p.m.

I got up, went and brushed my teeth, and put on a pair of flip-flops, all the time wondering why I agree to pick people up from the airport. It really is a ridiculous activity if you're not sleeping with the person. People in their thirties need to know that if they can't afford a taxi, then they don't deserve to go on a trip. I reminded myself to say this exact thought during one of my stand-up routines the next time Lydia came to a show; hopefully that would get the point across.

My vision still wasn't twenty-twenty, but I hoped that it would clear up once I got outside. I ran out the door and jumped into my dark blue Volvo. I drove to the end of the alleyway, then slammed on the breaks when I saw three young teenage girls wearing backpacks, crossing. I couldn't have been going more than five miles per hour since the entrance to the street was only a hundred feet from my space, but I'm sure I still scared the girls, so I lowered my window and leaned out. "I'm sorry, girls," I said as I waved.

"Fuck you, cunt," one of the girls responded, while the other two girls gave me the finger.

I couldn't believe my ears. These girls couldn't have been more than fourteen years old, and they were calling a complete stranger a cunt? I didn't even start using that word until my late twenties, and I curse all the time. Two of the girls were Mexican and one of them was white, but looked like she was trying very hard to be Mexican. In my opinion, pretending to be Mexican is right up there with wearing a mock turtleneck. Why would you *pretend* to be wearing a turtleneck?

By this time they had crossed over to the other side of the sidewalk, the side closest to my passenger door. I opened my car door and got out. "I'm sorry, did you just call me a cunt?" I asked the chunky Latina who had yelled it.

"That's right, fucking bitch, cuz that's what you are!" she yelled.

This was too much. I couldn't believe how anyone, never mind three young girls, could talk to a complete stranger like this. These girls were clearly walking home from school, which disturbed me even more. "I'm sorry . . ." I had to press on. "Where do you get off talking like that to complete strangers? How old are you?"

The girls had stopped where they were at this point, and the one I was talking to started walking back toward my car with her fingers and arms waving around like an orangutan. "Because that's what you fucking are," she replied. "A fucking cunt. How the fuck old are *you* is the better question, and where the fuck did you learn to drive?"

"Listen, you little bitch," I screamed, completely losing any remaining dignity that hadn't been lost earlier when I had inhaled more than five thousand calories in one sitting. "I didn't fucking hit your ass, and believe me it wasn't easy to miss, so I suggest you tone it down a notch. I was apologizing to you, and then you call me a cunt? Where are your parents?"

The girl was now standing on the other side of the car, still moving her head around in circles. "Who the fuck do you think you are, *asking* me about my parents? I know *you're* not my fucking mother, I know that! Shit!" Her girlfriends were now laughing as she turned around to join them. The fact that this girl wasn't backing down and had no qualms about talking to me like that—when in my mind, I thought I was being reasonable—pushed me over the edge.

Fully aware of my newfound upper body strength, I walked around the front of my car toward them and yelled, "Really? You're that tough that you can just yell at strangers? You think you're some sort of badass? Let's go," I said, shrugging my shoulders and bouncing from foot to foot with my fists clenched. "Let's do this!"

The fat girl seemed surprised by my reaction, as she should have been, knowing what I knew about my recent combat training. This little bitch was going to get what was coming to her. She was messing with the wrong person. A few months earlier I wouldn't have been able to defend myself in this way, but I tightened my abs, jumped up and down a couple of times, and got ready to rumble. She yelled something in Spanish, and then turned around and walked toward her friends. I, however, kept going.

"That's exactly what I thought. Think about it next time you want to shoot off your mouth!" Then, for good measure, I threw in a *"puta!"* I turned and walked back to my car, got in, and put my foot on the gas. That's when all three girls started running back toward my car, so I slammed on the brakes and got out again.

"Oh really?" I screamed. I stayed on my side of the car while the girls stopped where they were and all four of us assessed the situation. "This is ridiculous," I said, throwing my hands up, and went to get back into the car. Just as I did, all three girls took a few steps toward the car, and the wannabe Mexican girl kicked my passenger side door. That was the straw that broke the cameltoe's back.

I got out, and before I could even stand up, one of the girls was on the roof of my car, and the fat one had somehow managed to airlift herself to my side of the car and had a lock of my hair in her hands. Hair-pulling is a very painful experience, especially when your head is already pounding from an alarmingly volatile sugar misfire.

Shakira was pulling me out of the car by my hair when I decided the only way to release myself would be with a left upper-cut. Disappointingly, the fist I had formed landed directly in the center of my own forehead. The girl on top of the car was screaming, "Yeah, bitch," as the head Mexican took her one free hand and punched me in the stomach. Somewhere between that and the skinny girl spitting on me, it occurred to me that I was in a street fight and it was *not* going well.

My mind raced to remember all the new moves I had learned, but they were useless. I had spent most of my training with Brad fighting a punching bag that always stayed in the same position. I could fight a person who was standing still, but had no idea how to fight someone who was on the move.

I had to do something and I had to do it fast. I smacked the sloppy fat girl in the face, hard, and then punched her in the vagina, which resulted in her losing her grip on my hair. I ran as fast as I could, but only made it a few feet before one of my flip-flops dislodged and went flying into the air. I tripped and fell down, and just as I managed to get up and start running again, one of the girls kicked me in the ass, propelling me forward onto the pavement. Instinctively, I held both of my boobs together in order to cushion the fall. I scurried to my feet once more, and ran down the street in the opposite direction, all the while hearing the girls screaming, "Stupid cunt!"

Three blocks away, I found a bush and dove into it. After catching my breath while trying not to make too much noise, a couple of things crossed my mind: (a) This was not at all how I had planned on spending my afternoon; (b) My boxing classes had not paid off; and (c) I had a burning sensation over my left eye. I don't specifically remember getting struck in the eye, but everything happened so fast, there was a good chance that I had taken a punch.

It occurred to me that my brand-new Volvo was also sitting in the alleyway with the driver-side door open and the keys in the ignition. Obviously that would be gone. Either the girls would have stolen it, or someone else walking by would have stolen it. I didn't live in a bad neighborhood, but I knew that you didn't have a day like I was having and not get your car stolen. I was in a defeated state of mind and was feeling confused, not only about the direction my life had taken, but also about other things, like Lisa Rinna's career, and penguin birth.

Once I realized my Rollerblades were in my closet, and that I could use them to ride to the Santa Monica PD to file a police report, I had a moment of elation—until I remembered that my kneepads and helmet were in the trunk of my car. I had never actually worn a helmet before, but not having it handy gave me the perfect excuse not to be caught Rollerblading in public.

Then I remembered Lydia. "Fuck!" I ran back to my car as though in a drill I had seen in the movie *Sgt. Bilko*, where the soldiers bounced in and out of camouflage in order to avoid being seen by the assailants. Surprisingly, my car was still idling with the door wide open and the key still in it. No Mexicans to be seen or heard for miles. I hopped in, and carefully headed for the airport. My cell phone rang. It was Lydia.

"Yello?" I answered.

"Are you coming or what?"

"Yes, Lydia, I'm coming." I huffed. "I was jumped."

"Huh?"

"I said, I was jumped!"

"Chelsea, what are you talking about?"

"Jumped. You know . . . like, taken down by three girls at the same time. I was in a brawl!"

When I heard nothing on the other end, I said, "Lydia, do you copy?"

"Chelsea, what the fuck are you talking about? Jumped? This isn't a Michael Jackson video."

"I'll be there in fifteen minutes, and you'll see," I said as I hung up. Now I was pissed. As if I would make something like this up. The fact that I was still on my way to pick her ass up after being caught in a Holyfield/Tyson–like altercation made me feel like a really dedicated airport picker-upper, and the fact that she was not getting the significance of it infuriated me!

I couldn't wait for her to see my shiner and know that I had been involved in a full-throttle scuffle. "Homo you don't," I said as a gay man crossed the street in front of my car. "Homo you didn't!" I screamed again as he crossed slowly, all the while staring at me with a confused and disgusted look on his face. I was ready for another fight, and was pissed I had missed my golden opportunity to lay someone flat.

I arrived at LAX, and while I was pulling up to Continental Airlines, an officer told me to keep moving.

"I don't think so, buddy," I said, putting my car in park and stepping out. "You wanna piece of me?" I was pissed now, and no one was gonna fuck with me again.

"Excuse me?" he asked.

"You heard me, hotshot! You wanna rumble? You know what? I'm here to pick up my friend from the airport and I think it's ridiculous that we are not allowed to stop for one second to let her get in the car. Is my friend supposed to dive through the window while the car's moving?"

Lydia found me just as the officer was issuing me a ticket for parking my car, along with a second one for lewd behavior.

We didn't speak for most of the car trip home, until finally she turned and asked me, "What is wrong with you?"

"Um. Is that code for 'thanks for picking me up at the airport'?" I asked her.

"You have a huge knot in the middle of your forehead and your thirtieth birthday party is tomorrow night. How does that make you feel?"

"You know how it makes me feel, Lydia? It makes me feel like I'm mad as hell and I'm not gonna take it anymore!"

Lydia sighed loudly. I awaited her response with bated breath. I had finally taken a stand, and knew for sure my friends would have to see it my way. Someone, perhaps a higher power, was clearly out to get me.

Finally, without looking at me, she opened her mouth. "Please take surface streets."

CHAPTER ELEVEN

Mini-Me

I got an upsetting letter from the mother of a midget, who wrote that she had watched an interview of mine on television and, "as the mother of a little person, was deeply offended" by my comments regarding little people; above all, the fact that I referred to them as "nuggets."

What this woman doesn't understand is that I am not the enemy. Next to fat babies, midgets are my favorite things to hold. I love them so much, and I want to help them to do adult things like drive cars, Jet-Ski, and lip-synch. I'm in awe of their little limbs, their large craniums, and their medicine-ball asses. I love the little baby steps they take while shifting their weight from side to side, and the fact that when you knock one over accidentally, he flails like a turtle on its back that can't get up right away.

Let me make one thing clear: I do not have a midget fetish—I like to think of it as more of a healthy obsession. And because I adore them so much, I want to raise midget awareness and prevent their further exploitation by others. I am deeply offended by midget pornography and by people who hire midget strippers for bachelor parties. That type of behavior really crosses the line in my book. What I'm truly interested in is dressing them in evening wear, more along the lines of the attire Miss Piggy used to wear on the *The Muppet Show*, or the little man from Monopoly. I'm talking about tuxedos, sequined ball gowns, and fedoras.

More important, I'm interested in helping midgets realize that their height should never be a limitation. I want to challenge them with outdoor sports such as skydiving, bungee jumping, and water polo. To help them, I would also videotape these activities and review the footage with them afterward with some chalk and a pointer, much in the same vein as a football commentator. If a bunch of Elvis impersonators can get together and skydive out of a plane in groups, there is no reason midgets shouldn't be allowed that same opportunity. I can't explain where these feelings come from, and they are rivaled only by my deep affection for penguins. (The only difference being, once you catch a midget, they are much easier to hold on to.)

My midget fantasies were finally realized when I was on a hidden-camera television show called *Girls Behaving Badly*. In its fourth season the producers called me into their office and explained that a very cute midget had written in, begging to be on the show. "She's really cute and lives in Pittsburgh. We thought since your birthday is coming up, as your present, we'd fly her out to do a bit with you."

I couldn't believe my ears. "Let me see her," I demanded as I leaped over the chair that stood between me and my producer's computer screen. He opened the file and I nearly passed out. Her name was Kimmy and she looked just like me, but with smaller features. She had blond hair that was pulled back in a ponytail, was three-feet-eleven, and weighed fifty-two pounds. I know this because as soon as I got her on set, I immediately weighed and measured her.

The picture she sent showed her standing with one hand on her hip and one leg splayed out like a Rockette's. The other hand was holding a lit cigarette. She was wearing a pink leotard with light pink tights, through which I could make out five miniature toes on each foot that were eerily reminiscent of my favorite appetizer, popcorn shrimp.

"Two questions," I said, barely able to contain myself. "Can she stay at my house, and do I get to take her to a water park?"

A few weeks later the producers flew Kimmy to Los Angeles to be on the show. We decided we would incorporate her into a bit I did called "Officer Handy." This was a recurring character I played, a security officer who takes herself way too seriously and gives out citations to people for ridiculous reasons, such as not staying within the lines when crossing in a crosswalk, or speaking too loudly while shopping in a mall.

They flew Kimmy in the night before we started shooting, so the first time I saw her was on set. I made sure to get there bright and early that day, as I wanted to make a good impression. She walked in with our talent coordinator and squealed, "Hey, everyone!"

Kimmy was even more than I expected. She had on a pink T-shirt with a pair of pink jean shorts and pink high-top Nikes. I wondered whether she actually needed them for ankle support or if she was on a midget basketball team. It took everything in my power to hold myself back from launching out of my seat like a rocket and tackling her.

She was heading toward me, smiling and waving, and I stood up from my seat and kneeled down on one knee, bracing myself for a hug. My body's reaction was far stronger than I could have anticipated; I was magnetically drawn to Kimmy, mostly because of her little sausage fingers and Chicken McNugget toes. With arms spread wide open, I couldn't wait to squeeze her. My eyes were popping out of my head and I had the slow, steady look of a rattlesnake just about to strike a mouse.

"Hi, you crazy bitch!" she said as she ran into my embrace. "I fucking love you!"

This was music to my ears, as I already knew I felt love for her. I knew this was what a mother bear must feel after giving birth to a cub. I loved her even before I met her, and I would do everything in my power to see her in a tracksuit.

"I'm so happy you are here," I said as tears began to well up in my eyes. "Look at you!" I picked her up and spun her around to get a closer look at her ass. I stared at the back of her ponytail, trying to determine whether or not her hair was real or a clip-on.

"Don't you think we look identical?" I asked her as I kept spinning her around. Once I put her down, she took a couple of unsteady steps before she was able to gather her footing, and then she sat down. "Sorry, I'm a little dizzy."

Kimmy's best features were her head and triceps. She wasn't as fat as I would have liked, but she was extremely muscular, which made her shape very aerodynamic. I immediately started fantasizing about pinning a cape to her back and tossing her off the roof of my apartment building.

I didn't want to seem desperate by throwing myself at Kimmy. I had to play it cool. "Why don't you go get into wardrobe and I'll get you a script," I said. I had to approach this in the same way I would deal with a guy I was interested in: give her a little taste of me and then take off while she still wanted more.

The producers decided to have her play my deputy sheriff at a winery in downtown Los Angeles. How they grow grapes in a part of town that is mostly populated by gangs and high-rises is beyond me, but when alcohol is involved, I rarely ask questions.

The prank would take place during a routine wine tasting, with me pulling people over as they went from one tasting to another just three feet away—much like getting pulled over for a DUI, but on foot.

We dressed Kimmy up in a mini police woman's uniform that basically made me foam at the mouth. I have never in my entire life seen anything cuter. Not only was Kimmy the same size as my three-year-old nephew, she was also flat chested. Even though I had no intention of getting intimate with Kimmy, if I had my druthers, she would have had two cantaloupes taking the place of her mosquito bites.

I had a barrage of questions to ask her and had compiled a series of flash cards to remind me. For starters, where did she shop for clothes? Were her parents human-size? Were her tiny fingers able to handle a set of chopsticks? How many people had she been intimate with, and what were their shapes and sizes? Was she able to take showers? And last but not least, can two midgets produce a full-grown person?

We didn't have much time before the shoot, so I decided to hold off on my questions until after we were done. We went through the motions of what would take place. After I had questioned our unsuspecting victims as to how many glasses of wine they had consumed and what they intended on eating to soak it up, I would speak into my walkie-talkie, requesting backup. That would be Kimmy's cue to come charging onto the scene and help me give our victims a field sobriety test.

The plan was for her to enter through a side door, run under one of the tables the wine was on and slide through, finally landing at our feet. Then I would tell the victims that we had no choice but to give them a breathalyzer to check their alcohol level. At this point I would pick Kimmy up and hold her in front of a person, asking her to breathe into Kimmy's face. "She is trained to detect alcohol, not unlike a police dog," I would tell the person.

The first woman I pulled over was outraged. This was the

perfect type of person for our show. The more enraged she became, the funnier the bit was.

"Excuse me, Miss?" I asked as I pulled her away from a group of about eight patrons. "I'd like to ask you a couple of questions. First, I'd like to ask you for your license and registration."

"For what?" she asked, confused.

"Well, I'm Officer Handy, and this is my beat," I said, standing with my legs spread apart, gripping my nightstick. "I'd like to make sure you are not intoxicated."

"This is a wine tasting," she reminded me.

"Yes, I'm aware of that, but you seem to be enjoying your wine a little bit more than the crowd you're running with."

"Running with?" she asked, looking over at her friend, who was completely ignoring the fact that I was conducting an interrogation. He was the one who set her up to be on our show and had been instructed not to get involved. "I don't know any of these people," she said. "I'm just here with my friend."

"Never mind him," I said, referring to her friend and spreading my legs wider, with my arms crossed like the Terminator. "I'm going to need to know exactly how many drinks you've had since you arrived and how many you had before you got here."

"None!" she exclaimed, incensed. "I didn't drink anything before I got here. It's noon!"After a couple of minutes of me asking ridiculous questions about her driving record, I yelled into my walkie-talkie that I needed backup.

Kimmy then hauled ass through the side door, slid under

the table, and landed on top of my feet. The woman I was harassing was horrified as she looked down at my deputy. At this point I had to turn around to hide my laughter. We were in our fourth season of the show, and by this time I was having a hard time keeping a straight face during any of our filming. The jokes we were playing on people were becoming more and more ridiculous.

The woman didn't know what was happening and was getting angrier by the minute. "First of all," she said, "I am not intoxicated, and I don't appreciate coming to a wine tasting, where you are encouraged to drink, and then being pulled over by a security guard."

"Security officer," I corrected her.

"Whatever," she responded, still staring at Kimmy.

"Security officer!" I screamed as her shoulders jumped a little bit. I used this tactic on the show when people got indignant, and more often than not it succeeded, and I quickly regained control of the situation.

I grabbed Kimmy under her arms and lifted her up so that she and the woman were face to face. "Please exhale deeply into Deputy Kimmy's face," I ordered her. She looked at the group of people she had been separated from, who were now all watching. She took a deep huff and then blew into Kimmy's face.

"Again!" I ordered. I had to stall before I put Kimmy down because I was laughing so hard, and she was the only thing blocking me. She was heavier than I thought she'd be and my muscles were starting to atrophy. There was urine running down my leg inside my uniform, but I just had to accept it until I could compose myself. I realized rather quickly that that was never going to happen, so in order to not have our victim catch me laughing, I put Kimmy down suddenly and ran out of the room.

The next two people we played this joke on reacted much the same way, and I was finally able to keep it together for the third person. So far, this was the best day of my life.

After I had changed my underwear and we were done with the day's shoot, I told Kimmy that I was performing that night at The Comedy Store and that I would love for her to come. She was elated.

I picked her up at her hotel at 7 p.m. I was half hoping she was still in the police uniform she had worn during the shoot, but was also half wishing I could see her in a brand-new midget outfit. She came out to the car and climbed into the passenger side. She was wearing jeans that I had seen before at babyGap, her high-top sneakers, and a pink, rhinestone-studded tank top that was skintight, and barely covering either of her nipples. I was completely flabbergasted.

"Whoa, Kimmy. You're really serious about having a good time tonight," I told her, eyeing her tank top.

She started to laugh maniacally and said, "Girl, I have never been to a city like Los Angeles, and I am ready to rock!" Then she took out a Marlboro Red 100 that was twice the length of her fingers and lit it up.

She was a little firecracker and I loved it, but I also feared for her safety in such a revealing top. We headed toward a restaurant called The Stinking Rose, where I had made reservations after the hostess assured me they had high chairs.

The whole way to the restaurant, Kimmy went on and on about how grateful she was for my friendship and how this was by far the best experience of her life. Home life was not so good, she implied. I would have to wait until dinner before I pressed her for more details. This was just the way I imagined myself acting around Nancy Grace—available, yet distant.

Once we sat down at dinner, it didn't take me long to realize that I would gather more information than I could have ever bargained for. The waiter came over and she ordered a Captain Morgan and Coke.

"Are you even allowed to drink?" I asked her.

"Sure," she cackled, as she pulled out her ID for the waiter. Apparently, she was twenty-five.

"Wow, you look really young for your age," I told her.

"Thanks, Chelsea," she said. "I have to tell you, when I married my first husband, I wasn't even eighteen."

"What?" I blurted out. "Your first husband? How many husbands have you had?" I couldn't believe this little nugget was having grown-up sex, and I'd be lying if I didn't say I was horrified.

She went on to tell me that not only did she marry again, but her current husband was in prison for grand larceny. She lived with her mother, who has never accepted the fact that she married someone in prison.

"Wait a second," I interjected. "You met him while he was in prison?"

"Yes, but he got out right after we met," she told me. "But he ended up getting caught again. This time he didn't do it. He was framed."

"Of course he was," I said in complete agreement. The idea that Kimmy was involved in something as sophisticated as a framing was alluring. My mind ran the gamut of criminal possibilities, from espionage to high-level racketeering, until I was interrupted by Kimmy asking if she could borrow money to pay her phone bill.

I was a little thrown off guard, but told her that wouldn't be a problem. If this little spark plug wanted to squeeze me for a couple hundred bucks, that was fine with me. I was more intent on getting the waiter to take a picture of her sitting on my shoulders without causing too much of a stir.

Kimmy was on her third rum and Coke when she told me that she had almost all the money to bail him out, but was short one thousand dollars. "His trial isn't until the spring, so I want to get him out before then, just in case he ends up getting convicted."

I was beginning to become concerned with Kimmy's alcohol intake and asked her if her little body would be okay handling that much liquor.

"Oh, I get fucked up all the time," she said in a deeper voice than she had started the night with. The waiter came over and set down the tri-tip steak Kimmy had ordered. I was too nervous to eat and had only ordered a Caesar salad. I wanted to keep my hands free in case Kimmy needed me to cut her meat.

I squinted at her. "We still have to go to The Comedy Store, so maybe you should hold off on the booze."

She told me more about her mother, who was collecting money from the government for disability, and a father who had left home when she was three. I wanted to tell her to look on the bright side—she couldn't have changed that much in her condition, so at least he knew what she would look like twenty-two years later.

After Kimmy polished off her sixteen-ounce tri-tip, she asked me if I'd like dessert.

"You go ahead," I told her. "Anything you want." It was becoming pretty obvious that Kimmy probably didn't get out of her hometown much and that her life in Pittsburgh was pretty bleak. I started thinking of different ways that I could help turn her life around.

Maybe I could move her out to Los Angeles and we would start our own detective agency, or maybe I would just quit showbiz, move to Pittsburgh, and she and I would open an arcade. I wondered if she would eventually get on my nerves if we lived together.

I thought about all the fun baby pictures I could take of her and then send out to my relatives. We would go to the mall where people take their infants for pictures, and I would have her surrounded by ducks, pumpkins, or maybe holding a bat and baseball. Would she be opposed to sleeping in a planter? I didn't have the answers yet, but I knew my life would never be the same. I needed to help Kimmy and nothing was going to stop me.

After we finished dinner, the waiter obliged in taking a

picture of us. Wanting to avoid causing a scene, I simply walked around to her side of the table and picked up the booster seat she was sitting in. I held it next to my body—Kimmy and all—the same way a professional soccer player would hold the World Cup.

I helped her out of her booster seat and we walked to the car holding hands. Kimmy kept thanking me for her dinner the whole way to The Comedy Store.

I got there just as they were calling my name onstage, and I motioned for Kimmy to come with me.

"Come onstage with you?" she asked.

"Don't worry," I said. "You don't have to say anything, just follow me up, sit on the stool, and don't say a word. That will be funnier. Do you need help getting up there?"

"No," she said. "I'll climb it."

I got onstage with Kimmy following closely behind, and sure enough, she was able to wrangle herself to sit on top of the stool. I did my act and Kimmy would let out high-pitched squeals of laughter after every punch line. Other than that, I didn't refer to her once. When I was finished, I looked over and saw that Kimmy had maneuvered herself around and was on her stomach, sliding off the stool.

Once we were off the stage, Kimmy sped up and poked the side of my leg. "Get me another Captain and Coke. I'm going outside for a cigarette."

I got her drink and went outside to find her holding court with five male comics. She was standing in the center of the group, smoking a cigarette with one of her nipples fully exposed. Her speech was slurred as she explained to them that she had come out to Los Angeles to work on *Girls Behaving Badly*, and that she was only here for one night and wanted to make it count.

I walked over and pulled her shirt back over her nipple. I didn't like the way Mini-Me was carrying herself. Her hair was a mess and she wasn't too steady on her feet. Between slurred sentences, she'd laugh maniacally while her eyes rolled back into her head.

"Kimmy," I said, hiding her drink behind my back. "Are you ready to go back to your hotel?"

"No fucking way, are you kidding?" she shot back. "I'm just getting started. You can leave if you want to."

As if I was just going to leave my little doppelgänger alone at a comedy club, surrounded by a group of male comics. I didn't even want to think about all the horrible things that could happen to her.

"Kimmy, I am not leaving you," I told her.

"I'm twenty-five years old, for Christ's sake," she told me as the guys all started laughing. One of the comics offered to give her a ride home.

"I don't think so," I replied gruffly, and then turned back to Kimmy. "I'm not kidding, we need to go now."

"Fuck off!" she yelled, and then fell back into the ledge of plants behind her.

Now this was turning into blatant disrespect. I had not raised Kimmy to behave like this, and I didn't know what kind of discipline was appropriate for a nugget. Would I just give her a time-out, or would I have to opt for a full-blown pants-down spanking?

"Listen, Kimmy, I am not leaving here without you. So you can either walk with me over to my car on the count of three, or there is going to be big trouble."

Her next move was to pull her tank top down in the middle of her chest, exposing both of her nipples. I walked over to her, picked her up underneath her arms, put her on my hip, and headed for the car. All the while, she was kicking and screaming. I got to my car, opened my door, and threw her into the car seat I had rented.

Now Kimmy was crying. This made me feel terrible, but fortunately, right before Kimmy's arrival, I had read *What to Expect When You're Expecting,* and knew I could not let her manipulate me with tears. I had to remain strong. "Kimmy, please don't cry. Please. What about if we get you some ice cream?"

"I'm thorry," she slurred. "I'm tho thorry. You have been tho nithe to me, and I had the beth day today of my life, and I juth don't want it to end."

"I understand that," I told her. "But you are wildly intoxicated and I really think you need to go to bed. You can barely stand up straight."

I pulled out of the parking lot as she kept repeating herself over and over again. "I'm tho thorry. . . .You are tho nice. . . . I'm tho drunk."

We pulled up to her hotel and she was still crying as she hugged me good-bye. One of the valets came over and I asked him to make sure she got up to her room safely. He took one look at her and flashed me the A-okay sign. I wrote down her address and told her I would send her the pictures we'd taken of me weighing her at the winery. As she was sliding out of the passenger seat, she turned back with tears streaming down her face and asked, "Can I get fifty bucks?"

At this point logic should have set in and I should have recognized a pattern. I, of course, was like a wife who keeps getting backhanded by her husband, but instead chooses to focus on the fact that he brings home a steady income.

I didn't have that much cash left, so instead I wrote her a check. I threw in an extra twenty-five for good measure.

When I woke up the next morning the cloudiness that had taken over my brain the night before had dissipated, and I was finally starting to think clearly. I knew what had to be done: I had to raise money to get Kimmy's husband out of the clinker.

I got dressed, drove directly to the production office of our show, and made everyone chip in.

The only resistance I got was from our line producer, Sam, who looked at me like I asked him for money to support Tonya Harding's return to figure skating. "You must be fucking kidding me," he said. "I'm not giving that little bitch a dime. That bitch is a con artist if there ever was one, and you must be a fucking idiot."

Not only was I horrified by the blasphemy of Sam's accusation, I felt like someone had punched me in the stomach, and reacted as such. "Pipe the fuck down!" I told him as I took a few steps in his direction, with one finger pointing in his face and the other in my jacket pocket, trying to make it look like I might be carrying a pistol. "You are going to give me money, you cheap shit, and you might want to think about what kind of damaging things you say before you ruin someone's reputation. She is just a baby."

"No, Chelsea, she is not a baby; she's twenty-five and she's a victim. I've seen people like her before and she's full of shit. And the fact that you are stupid enough to fall for it is really disappointing. I thought you were smarter than that."

I was offended that my intelligence was being called into question, but even more appalled by the way Sam was talking about a small child.

"You would never talk that way about a full-grown woman," I told him as I stormed out. It disturbed me on many levels to think that Kimmy, someone who could just have easily been born in my shoes, or me in hers, wasn't getting the support she deserved. There were so many similarities between us, and I felt it was my duty to help her achieve the most that a short life expectancy had to offer.

I ended up collecting $476 from the rest of the crew and then threw in $200 of my own money. I wanted to give her more, but was also saving up to adopt a highway, and knew I had to act responsibly.

I sent Kimmy a cashier's check for $676, assuming she probably didn't have a checking account, and waited for her call to thank me. The call never came. Three months later I got Kimmy's contact information from our production manager and called her mother, who informed me that not only was Kimmy's husband still in jail, but Kimmy had taken off to Costa Rica with the money I sent her and was now working as a scuba instructor.

I hung up the phone and sat down, stupefied. It wasn't that she lied about what she intended to do with the money. What really got my goat was that after everything we had been through together, she had never once mentioned to me that she could swim. I would have *killed* to see that.

CHAPTER TWELVE

Costa Rica

I woke him up at 3:30 a.m. I walked into his room, looked at the black pair of boxer shorts he was sporting, decorated with swiss cheeses that had smiley faces, and repeated the phrase "Dad" four times until his arm spasmed and smacked me on the side of the head.

"Get up," I said, and walked out of the room, cradling the left side of my face. My mother had passed away a few months earlier, and I was taking my father, or as I affectionately like to call him, "Bitch Tits," to Costa Rica for two weeks with my friend Shoniqua and her mother, Latifa. I was expecting to bond with my father on this trip. What I wasn't expecting was for people to think we were a couple.

His descent down a flight of stairs makes the same sound a gorilla would make if he came upon a staircase, except that a gorilla would make better use of its arms and legs. Slow, deliberate, and confused is the best way to describe his gait. Stairs require him to negotiate his weight from one foot to the other while also steadying his corpulent frame with one hand on the railing and one hand on the wall. Due to the arduousness of the task, he makes sure only to come down once in the morning and to go up once at night.

After he took five minutes to walk down ten steps, and then a smaller set of five steps leading into the kitchen, I watched him sidle up to the medicine cabinet and take one pill each out of fourteen separate bottles. After he had compiled his collection, he placed each of the seventy-five pills into a white, letter-sized envelope, licked and sealed it, and then placed it in his back pocket.

"Are you planning on mailing those to someone?" I asked him.

Without responding to my question, he barked for me to get his pill bag out of the hallway. Bitch Tits's pill bag turned out to be a red duffel bag large enough to carry a golden retriever. I looked outside and saw a black Town Car in the driveway with its headlights on.

"Do you have a toiletry kit?" I asked, thinking of his shaving supplies and oral hygiene accoutrements that I would surely be overseeing.

"I use a towel."

Excluding one trip to the Dominican Republic that my mother had strong-armed him into the previous year, he hadn't been out of the United States since their honeymoon forty-seven years earlier. Prior to that trip, he claims to have traveled all over the world, but only by boat. He talks incessantly about how he lived in several different countries and is constantly announcing that he speaks eight languages. If saying, "hello," "good-bye," and "thanks for nothing," constitutes being fluent in a different language, then I speak three: English, Hebrew, and Jive.

Bitch Tits opened our front door to find the driver standing there. *"Hola, señor. ¿Como estás?"*

The driver, who looked like he was straight out of *The Sopranos*, looked quizzically at my father and replied, *"¿Bueno?"*

"Dad, we're not in Costa Rica yet. Cool it with the Spanish."

After we arrived at the airport and checked our larger bags, we came upon the metal detector and were abruptly stopped on the other side by a large black woman with penciled-in eyebrows and fingernails long enough to fight off a porcupine. She held up my father's red duffel bag and asked if she could search it. I told her yes and looked at my father, who threw his hands up as if he was being asked to submit to an anal cavity search and exclaimed, "Do what you gotta do. I don't know what you think you're going to find!"

Seconds later, the female security officer grabbed a pair of my father's shorts from the top of the duffel bag and emptied out the contents of his pockets. A lighter, three nail files, a pocket wrench, a pair of pliers, a screwdriver, and a nectarine fell onto the folding table. I looked at the woman, looked at my father, and then looked around to see if anyone else was watching.

"What's the problem?" my father asked the woman.

"Sir, I'm going to have to take this lighter away from you," she said.

"The lighter?" I asked her. "What about the bomb kit he's carrying around? He could do a lot more damage to a person with that wrench."

"I need the wrench!" he shrieked.

"For what?" I asked.

"What if something goes wrong with the plane?"

The woman put everything back in his bag except the lighter. Three miles later, we found our gate.

"Well, this is a joke," he huffed as he sat his oversize body down. "What kind of airport is this, with gates miles away from the entrance? It's a good thing I had that quintuple bypass surgery last year."

Good for who? I wondered. "Dad, why don't you go up to the ticket counter and try to get us upgraded?"

My father has about as much shame as Star Jones and, being the Jew that he is, loves to get something for nothing. My negotiating skills are on par with George Bush's reading ability. And, just like Dubya, every time I've tried to put forth an effort, I am reminded that my only true strength lies in drinking.

I was engrossed in an issue of *Us Weekly* when my father sauntered back over to where I was sitting and sat down without saying a word. Just as they started boarding I heard my name over the loud speaker, and with a huge smile on her face, the woman handed my father and me our first-class tickets. "Wow, Dad, I'm impressed."

"Quiet, don't say anything," he said through clenched teeth as he poked me in the ribs. "Just smile."

There were twelve seats in first class. Nine of them were empty, and the only other person in the section was a black man wearing three large gold chains. After my father barked something in Spanish at the male flight attendant, he turned to the black man covered in gold jewelry and said, "Where ya' headed, Q-Tip?"

Bitch Tits primarily watches two networks—CNN and MTV. The only thing he'll turn Christiane Amanpour off for is *Total Request Live*, or, as he and Justin Timberlake refer to it, *TRL*.

"Dad," I said pleadingly while looking over at the black man seated across from us. "I'm sorry. He's retarded."

"I wouldn't say that," my father jumped in.

"I would."

"Well, retardation is a very serious affliction and no one has ever confused me with being one."

"With being what?" I asked.

"A retard, Chelsea. Please try and follow the conversation."

I realized that this flight alone could send me over the edge, so I took an Ambien out of my purse, bit it in two, swallowed my half, and dropped the other half in the orange juice Bitch Tits had just been handed.

Five hours later we were landing in San José. I slipped off my eyeshades to find my father with his bowling-ball head resting on his shoulder and a steady flow of drool coming out of his mouth and pooling on his stomach, where most of the contents spilling out of his mouth usually end up.

"Geez, I don't know what the hell happened," he slurred, completely out of sorts. "One minute I was awake and the next minute I was zapped, just like that," he said as he tried to snap his fingers, but he was too disoriented to make the necessary connection between his middle finger and thumb. *"¡Me gusta agua!"* he yelled out to the flight attendant and then turned to me. *"¿Te gusta agua?"*

"I don't speak Spanish."

"Oh, for Christ's sake!" he yelled. "Do you want some water or don't you?"

"No."

I could tell already that listening to my father speak Spanish for the entire trip was going to get really irritating. The only advantage I could think of was that I wouldn't be able to communicate with him.

"Hey, Chels," he said as he shoved his Lacsa Airline map into my lap. "You were wondering where Costa Rica is located, and here it is. Right between Nicaragua and Panama. Your lack of geographical knowledge is truly astounding."

"Well, I am an American, and we're pretty stupid," I reminded him. "Besides, I knew Costa Rica was in a general southerly direction from Mexico; I just didn't know where exactly."

"Sometimes, Chelsea, I really wonder how you get by from day to day. It's a good thing you're voluptuous."

"At least I asked where it was," I said. "And please don't

refer to me as voluptuous. Can you please go back to speaking Spanish?"

Just as I turned to look out the window, the flight attendant handed my father a bottle of champagne and grabbed my hand. "Congratulations, dear. I'm sure the two of you will have a wonderful life together."

It took a full minute of hand-holding with a perfect stranger to realize we had been upgraded to first class due to them thinking my father and I were on our honeymoon . . . because that's what my father told them. This was my first trip alone with my father, and so far, I wasn't having a good time.

Once in Costa Rica, we rolled off the airplane and through customs without any major setbacks. I was in charge of carrying my father's passport, which isn't much more reassuring than giving it to an illegal alien. We walked outside into the smoldering heat while fifteen local taxi drivers gathered around us, yelling things in Spanish.

Then a homeless man with a dog approached us and put his hand out. This happens to be something that I have a real problem with: homeless people with pets who approach you for food. How can they have the nerve to beg for food when they have a perfectly delicious dog standing right there? I didn't care if this guy understood English or not. "Tell me when you're out of dog, buddy. Then we can talk about splitting a falafel."

I heard someone yell "Papa Handler!" from across the street and looked over to see Shoniqua waving her arms at us. Her mother was parked on a bench beside her, looking like she had just given birth to a water buffalo.

"There she is!" my father exclaimed. "How's my Black Magic?" he said, dropping his duffel bag and suitcase next to me and crossing the street, stopping traffic. I picked his bags up and stumbled over to where they were standing. They were embracing each other like mother and child penguins.

My father loves Shoniqua because she can listen to him talk for hours on end. But mostly he likes her because they both share the belief that the less money they spend, the better. They met when she and I were on a television show together years earlier, and their fondness for each other was based on the fact that they are the two cheapest people I have ever met in my life. My father also revels in the fact that, by having a relationship with Shoniqua, he is somehow in with the black community.

Her mother, Latifa, had never met my father before, and when he went in for a kiss on the cheek, he somehow managed to spray the entire side of her face with his saliva. Latifa grimaced, looked at me with her glasses pulled down on her nose, and without whispering said, "Well, that was disgusting."

I've known Latifa for as long as I've known Shoniqua, and consider her to be my black mother. Mostly because I only have one black friend, and Latifa is her mother. She has raised ten children of her own, has fostered more than a hundred other children, and runs a childcare center. She supplements this income with donations from Shoniqua, myself, and anyone else stupid enough to give money away to someone just because they ask for it. "It's fucking hot," she said as she wiped her forehead.

My father started speaking Spanish to one of the drivers

and before I knew it we were in a cab on the way to a smaller airport, where we had to take a puddle jumper from San José to Tambor. We pulled up to a single-engine, five-seater plane.

"What the fuck is this?" Latifa muttered upon seeing the size of the plane. My father's head jerked around with wide eyes upon hearing the word "fuck" come out of her mouth.

"It's a private plane we have to take to Tambor," I told her.

"Nobody said any motherfucking thing about a private plane."

"The language!" Melvin said, looking shocked. "This one's worse than you, Chels."

"Mama, I told you we had to take a little plane; driving there would take eight hours and a one-hour boat ride," Shoniqua told her.

"I love boats," my father declared.

I walked my father, who didn't take his eyes off Mama Latifa, over to the seat next to the pilot, assuming that was the only seat with enough room to fit him. The pilot and I helped him step up into the seat, and after trying to get his seat belt around his stomach for a full two minutes, I gave up and walked to the other side of the plane to sit down.

"Hold up," Shoniqua said. "When are we going to check in with the embassy?"

I looked at her and then looked back out the window, shaking my head.

"Chels, I'm serious. We need to check in with the embassy. What if our asses get kidnapped?"

"Shoniqua, you are six feet tall with an ass the size of a

giraffe. Who the hell is going to kidnap you? And furthermore, I doubt there is an embassy where we're going."

"First of all, bitch, my ass has gotten a lot smaller since I started acupuncture."

"Fine," I replied exhaustedly. "A baby giraffe."

"That's better. And of course there's an embassy. Every country has an embassy."

"Yeah, I know that, but they're not usually on the beach."

"Listen, if one of these little Costa Ricans fucks around and tries to get my ass, don't think for a second I won't fork the motherfucker." Apparently, along with my father's bag of artillery, the dinner fork that Shoniqua travels with everywhere in case of an attack also managed to make its way through airport security.

The plane took off with about as much control as a white-water raft in a Category Five hurricane. I put my headphones on and stared out the window, trying not to vomit.

Forty minutes later, the plane started its descent and, from what I could tell, looked like it was headed for a landing strip not much bigger than the ones you see in *Playboy*.

"You have got to be fucking kidding me," Latifa said with a moan, looking out the window.

Minutes later we were on the ground. We were greeted by a young Costa Rican boy who led us all to his mini-SUV. Right before my father got in, he walked ten feet away to a tree, turned his back to us, and peed.

"Shit, I gotta go too," Latifa said as she hopped out of the car in the direction of another tree and squatted behind it.

"Well, looks like we got a pair of fuckin' winners here," Shoniqua said. "These two must have been separated at birth."

The dirt road leading us to Santa Teresa couldn't have been more bumpy if we were driving through the outback in a rickshaw. Ten minutes into the ride, I grabbed my carry-on bag, rifled through it until I found two sports bras, and put them both on over my shirt. During this time, my father and the driver were deep in a Spanish conversation, with the driver hysterically laughing at everything my dad was saying—a clear sign that he couldn't understand a word of it.

An hour later we arrived in Santa Teresa, and pulled up to the two villas I had rented. The villas were one hundred feet apart from each other in front of a beach, and separated by several dirt paths and what looked like a mini rain forest. At least a dozen dogs gathered around our taxi, wagging their tails.

"If one of these motherfucking dogs comes near me, I'm gonna kick him in the fucking neck," Latifa mumbled.

"Relax, will ya?" my father said as he craned his neck back to look at her. "These dogs aren't going to do anything to you, they're all half-breeds. Look at 'em. That one in front of the car looks like he's got a little horse in him."

Isabel, the property manager, greeted us and gave us a tour of the two villas. Each one had two bedrooms, a kitchen, a bathroom, and a sitting room that looked out onto the beach. Each villa was beautifully crafted from the most gorgeous wood I had ever seen and, once you got upstairs, hot as fucking hell.

"I'm going to need a cocktail," I told my father as I came back downstairs covered in sweat.

Isabel was in my father's room showing him how to turn on the air conditioning, which was only available in the master bedroom of each villa. Upon discovering this information, I spent the next thirty to thirty-five seconds considering sleeping in the same bed as my father. I wondered if it would be possible to avoid any and all physical contact if I slept on top of the covers and positioned myself at just the right angle. It seemed plausible, but after serious consideration, it was not a risk I was willing to take.

After settling in, we collected the girls, and the four of us made the three-minute trek along the beach to the "hotel" that Isabel had recommended for lunch. The "hotel" consisted of four bungalows, a swimming pool, six tables looking out over the pool onto the ocean, and fifteen Costa Rican gardeners. The one thing I could tell for sure was that Costa Ricans are very serious about their gardening.

Four hours later we were on our fourth pitcher of the best margaritas I have ever tasted and about two drinks away from making a four-person pyramid. My father has never been a big drinker, and I've certainly never witnessed him having a margarita, never mind eight of them. Latifa really starts to loosen up after a couple of drinks, and in the past hour had used the word "pussy" three times, and followed that up with her theory that men are good for one of two things: "dick or money."

Bitch Tits sat there frequently widening his eyes and

elbowing me in the ribs, as if we were at a live concert performance or the circus. It's very rare to see my father so quiet, as he has a very high opinion of his own opinion and loves to share it with anyone who is breathing. To see Mama Latifa having such an intimidating effect on him was more than mildly amusing. Only upon hearing Latifa's assessment about men and dick or money could he contain himself no longer.

"Well, I think that's a bit of an overstatement," he said, crossing his arms with the same seriousness a congressman would use when trying to pass a new law.

"Shit." Latifa moaned. "I didn't get ten kids from not knowing what men are good for, that's for sure."

"You got that right, Mama," Shoniqua chimed in as they high-fived each other.

"Well, Papa Handler, why don't you tell me what your forte is?" Latifa asked.

"Well, that's private, darling," my father said in a very flirtatious tone—one he unfortunately usually reserves for my sisters and me.

"I know you got that summer house in Martha's Vineyard, so I guess that answers which you're good for," she said, inferring that my father was either bad in bed, or wasn't well endowed. I didn't know which was more nauseating: the thought of my father having sex, or the thought of my father having a small penis.

"Let me tell you girls something," he said as a gob of spit flew out of his mouth and landed in my eye. "My wife was a very passionate woman, and she and I would make love for days." Then he raised his voice so all six of the other people in the restaurant could hear too, and repeated, "Days! We would go for days, and—"

"I'm going to bed," I said as I got up and headed for where we were staying.

"She really needs to relax. Let her go to bed and sleep it off. She's very stressed out," I heard him tell them as I walked away.

I walked back to the villa, popped another Ambien, and sent off an e-mail to my brothers and sisters.

> DAY #1
>
> Shamu and I have arrived safely in Costa Rica. He was stopped by airport security because he carries enough artillery in his pants pockets to construct a sawed-off shotgun. Evidently, he thought we were headed to Iraq.
>
> I just left him at dinner with Shoniqua and her mother, who he now calls Black Magic and Black Magic's Mama. For the third time today, he has referenced his love-making with Mom, and the only respite I see from these conversations is to physically tape his mouth shut. I will have to ask him how to ask for duct tape in Español.
>
> His head seems to have gotten bigger. Not sure if it's swollen from the plane ride. I will keep you apprised of all new developments.

The following morning I woke up at around eight thirty and looked out the window to see the back of my dad's thirty-pound head. He was sitting in one of the Adirondack chairs in front of the beach, holding up binoculars, with three dogs lying next to him. I put on my bathing suit and walked over to where he was sitting.

"How these surfers come out of the water after partaking in such a beautiful sport and then light a miserable cigarette is point-blank astonishing," he said without looking at me. I looked over in the direction his binoculars were focused to see what he was talking about.

"Dad, that isn't a cigarette," I said as I saw the guy pass what he was smoking to his girlfriend. "It's a joint."

"Oh, is it?" he said, putting down his binoculars. "Well, that I can understand."

"Oh, really? That you understand?"

"It's the reefers. Everybody here loves to smoke the reefers. I just had breakfast at the little Rastafarian joint next door. Beautiful girl working there, like a goddess; she smokes the reefers too. By the way," he said, looking me up and down, "you look very sexy in your little swimsuit."

"You already had breakfast?" I asked him.

"That's right," he replied.

"By yourself?"

"Of course by myself!" he exclaimed. "I am an adult, you know. Black Magic and her mother aren't up. Those two were up yappin' until two in the morning. Shoniqua's mother's really got a mouthpiece on her. And Shoniqua, oh jeez! She's got one story after another story, and then there's another story. Those two can talk each other under the table."

"I'm surprised you were quiet long enough to hear anything."

"Oh, please," he snorted. "Like I could get a word in edgewise. By the way, tomorrow is Father's Day. I don't know what you have planned, but I'd like some swordfish." Then he barked something in Spanish to the dogs. "These dogs only respond to Spanish." One of the dogs looked up, while the other two made absolutely no movement. "This one's trying to make a name for himself. Follows me wherever I go. Not a good-looking dog, but what are you gonna do? How did you sleep?" he asked, and before I could answer, interrupted me. "The ocean is like a symphony, Chelsea. The waves undulating in and out, then back in again, it's like a beautiful symphony. Do you know what I mean by symphony?"

"I'm going to make some coffee," I said, and turned to walk back to the villa. Two minutes later he walked in and slowly made his way upstairs to the kitchen. "I'd like some decaf," he declared once he reached the top.

"There is no decaf."

"Well, then, half-and-half."

"Half and half of what?" I asked him.

"Half coffee, half cream, same thing as decaf. I've been thinking," he went on. "I want you to take a picture of that tree, Chelsea." I turned and saw him standing next to my bed, holding up his binoculars to look at a tree that you could touch if you put your hand out the window. "I want pictures of all the trees around here. This one right here is just about three hundred years old."

"How do you know it's not just two hundred years old?"

"You can tell by looking at the base of the tree. The width of the base, Chelsea! That tree is coming up on its three hundredth birthday, goddammit!" You'd think I'd asked him if a vagina could be used as a pencil sharpener. "Go ahead, take a picture, for crying out loud," he ordered as I emptied coffee grounds into the coffee maker.

"In a minute," I said, gesturing that both my hands were occupied.

"I've got a question for you, Chels," he said, lowering himself into an armchair. "Have you ever thought of getting some lowlights?"

Day #2

"The ocean is like a symphony" is Dad's new catchprase, along with "surfer's paradise"—and coming in third is still his old standby, "Arabs are the scum of the earth."

After I made him coffee, he said he was going swimming and had plans for lunch. We've been here for less than twenty hours and he already has lunch plans with the female Italian landscaper. He said it's good to brush up on his languages. I was tempted to ask the landscaper how to say "shut the fuck up" in Italian.

There are several dogs on the grounds who are all following Dad around. "Dogs love me, even these half-breeds.

Keep 'em away from Shoniqua and that mother of hers, though. These dogs do not like blacks."

Shoniqua's mother used the *n* word after four forty-ounce Coronas last night, and Dad, who was appalled, said, "Black Magic Mama, please don't use language like that. I prefer *schvartzeah*."

If any of you want to come here, everything is paid for.

Once my dad returned from lunch, he passed out in his bedroom and didn't wake up for four hours. Going for a swim earlier had completely exhausted him. And it occurred to me that in order for me to get any writing done, it would be necessary to get him swimming every day to completely wipe him out. It seemed to me that caring for a seventy-five-year-old wasn't much different than caring for a toddler. Once they go down for a nap, it's important to get as much done as possible.

At around seven my father walked into Shoniqua's villa, where I was having a cocktail with the girls, and proclaimed, "It's time to eat."

"Hi, Papa Handler!" Shoniqua exclaimed, running over to give him a kiss.

Latifa slurped down the remains of her forty-ounce Corona, grabbed another, and the four of us walked over to our new favorite restaurant. The same waitress from the night before came over, and before she had a chance to even say "hello," Bitch Tits announced, "I'd like some swordfish."

"Dad, we haven't even ordered drinks yet and no one has even looked at the menu. Will you please take it down a notch?"

"I'm sorry," the waitress said. "We don't have swordfish."

"Margaritas," my father said, staring at the table. Apologizing for my father had become part of my daily routine early on in life, as he makes a point of having no social skills whatsoever. This is a man who can give you the meaning of any word in the dictionary, the history of any war that has ever taken place, the geographical location of any city in the world, but has never in his life learned the words "please" or "thank you."

"You look good in red, Papa Handler," Shoniqua said, admiring the shirt he had put on for dinner.

"Do you think so?" he asked, turning his head and looking at her sideways. "Chelsea and my wife always liked me in red. Red, yellow, and chartreuse. You know, my wife was many things," he said, apparently picking up in the middle of a conversation no one else was having. "She was an artist, a painter, a carpenter, an engineer; she could sew, she was a mechanic, a cook, a baker, a lover, a painter, a gardener, a landscaper, a mother, a daughter, a sister, an aunt, an uncle, a volunteer . . ."

"Okay, Dad, she wasn't an uncle."

"Chelsea," he said. "You really need to relax. You seem very stressed out."

"I'm gonna get me some filet mignon," Mama Latifa announced. "You're paying, right, Chelsea?"

"Of course she's paying," my father replied.

"Dad, do you want to split a salad as an appetizer?" I asked him.

"I'll take my own salad, and then I'll take the ribs," he

replied as a mango fell off the roof of the restaurant and split open on the ground.

"They're not going to have ribs, Dad."

"Of course they will. What restaurant doesn't have ribs?"

The waitress came over with the menu, which was written on a chalkboard and was different each day and, of course, did not include ribs.

"Goddamn bugs are eating me alive," Mama Latifa said, smacking herself in the arm.

"I know," the waitress responded. "It's awful right now with the bugs; it's actually the worst time of year. My legs are in terrible shape."

We all looked at her exposed legs, which looked like she had gotten caught in a minefield. More than once. Both her legs were covered in awful, blistering sores.

"Jesus Christ!" my father yelled, looking down at them. "You better take a seat."

She smiled and went on to tell us that her skin is extra-sensitive to the bites, and that there was a fatal reaction she could have if the bites got any worse.

"Well, you better pack your bags and get the fuck out of Costa Rica!" Shoniqua said.

"I know, I should totally leave for the off-season, but I just love it here."

"Well, you're not gonna love it if your ass is dead," Mama Latifa added.

The notion that this girl could potentially die from mosquito bites, and was only mildly concerned about it, made me think she was probably one of those girls who wouldn't put up a fight against a rapist. I always thought that if I were ever to get raped, I would try and get along with my rapist. Maybe ask him what kind of music he likes, would he like a cocktail, that sort of thing. Just to try and make it as civilized as possible. And then right before we started to make love, I would just tell him I have herpes, AIDS, and/or gonorrhea.

"Listen, Hilary," my father said to the waitress. "You're what my daughter refers to as a 'hot mess.' What you need is vinegar for those bug bites. I've got some at the house if you don't have any here."

"Vinegar? Really?" She asked confused. "Balsamic?"

"No," my father replied, losing all patience. "Not balsamic, for crying out loud, you're not a salad. White vinegar. If you don't have it, Chels will go back to the villa and get mine. I'll administer it."

More great news. I grabbed a flashlight and limped back through the woods to get vinegar. When I came back, covered in sweat from the humidity, my father was, of course, talking about what a ravenous sex drive my mother had. Mama Latifa was sitting up at the table, sleeping with her mouth open. Two seconds later, her head jerked forward and her eyes popped open. Then she reached into her mouth, removed her top teeth, and put them on the table. "Nothing like a man who loved a woman, Melvin," she slurred. "Nothing like it." Then it started pouring.

Day #3

Last night there was a torrential downpour at dinner, so we had to navigate our way through the woods in pouring rain with Dad traveling at his fastest gait (1 1/2 mph) and me holding Latifa's teeth. All of us hung out in Shoniqua's villa listening to hip-hop for an hour before Dad said, "I'd like to hear some Shakira."

Shoniqua's mother was dancing around Dad, shaking her ass, and he, of course, thinks she has a crush on him. I told them I was going to the bathroom around ten, and instead came back to our villa to pass out.

I heard doors slamming when Dad came home and I looked at the clock. It was 1:30 a.m. Today he said he's "hungover."

The girls apparently convinced him last night that he is part black due to his "negrolike" features—his "nigger lips" and his wide nose. When I asked dad not to use the *n* word, he told me, "They said it, not me! They said the *n* word. I would never use a word like that." Then he spent the rest of this morning talking about how he thinks that's a huge compliment, coming from two colored girls.

"Happy Father's Day," I said, handing my dad a plate of scrambled eggs and a cup of half and half with a splash of coffee. He was seated in his usual spot in one of the Adirondack chairs, with the three dogs that follow him around lying at his feet.

"Good morning, love," he said, taking the plate and coffee

from me as if it was completely normal for me to be making him breakfast. "I'll tell you, those girls are something. Black Magic and her mother. That mother can talk a blue streak. You know what these eggs are missing, Chels? Paprika."

I looked at my father, wondering how my mother could have listened to this for forty-seven years. I couldn't believe that I had defended him so many times to her. I just knew my mother was sitting up in heaven watching my father order me around like a slave and laughing her ass off.

"They don't have that here, Dad. How about nothing?"

"You know, black people have a whole race issue going on among themselves. They don't like the ones that are too dark. The lighter the skin, the more beautiful they are considered."

"That's exactly right, Dad—especially if you're a racist."

"No, Shoniqua told me last night. Chocolate brown and lighter are the most desirable shades. . . . It's a little late for them to be sleeping, don't you think?"

"Well, you didn't come home until one thirty. It's only nine. They sleep late."

"I don't care if they sleep all day. That's their prerogative," he said while shoving forkful after forkful of eggs into his mouth. "You think you're pretty sneaky, don't you, Chels?"

"How's that?" I asked.

"Oh, you know what I'm talking about. Don't think I don't know what you're trying to do, bringing Mama Latifa here on vacation with us. I am not looking for a steady girlfriend," he said, banging one fist on the arm of his chair. "I am not equipped to perform in that capacity anymore. She's only fifty-two, and women that age are still in their prime and looking for penetration. She obviously has a crush on me."

"Dad, I don't mean to burst your bubble, but I don't think Latifa is interested in being penetrated by you." Once again, I found myself having a conversation about sex with my father.

"Listen to me, Chelsea. Women are all the same. JLo, Britney Spears, Missy Elliot. These women all expect a lot of physical performance."

"I'm going swimming," I said.

"Look at that body! Hot stuff tonight!" he yelled as I walked toward the water. Two surfers on the beach turned to see who was yelling obscenities at me while I hung my head low and avoided any eye contact.

I was in the water for three minutes when I heard three short abrupt whistles, followed by two longer ones that sounded like a foghorn. I looked back toward Bitch Tits and saw him waving for me to come ashore. I got out of the water and walked the fifty feet to where my father was perched.

"Where did you get a whistle?" I asked him.

"Stay where I can see you," he said, holding the whistle that was now covered in scrambled eggs. Then he got to his feet, shuffled over to where I was standing, and turned away from me. "Give me a scratch on the back."

"No thanks," I responded.

"Chelsea, it's Father's Day."

Scratching my father's back isn't something I take immense pleasure in doing. The most vile part of this procedure is that he pulls up his shirt so that I can make direct contact with his skin. My father's body and skin, along with the entire cast of *The Golden Girls*, is definitely something that should be kept under wraps at all times.

The back-scratching combined with my father yelling "Hot stuff tonight!" and "Look at that body" every time I walked by him in a bikini would lead anyone to believe that we were dating. I kept making sure to say the word "dad" loudly whenever one of the gardeners walked by, even when my father was nowhere in sight.

One of the dogs got up and followed my father to where he was standing.

"This one follows me everywhere I go. He probably smells Whitefoot." Our dog, Whitefoot, had died four months earlier, the day after my mother passed away. People say that pets can sense when one of their owners is dead, and I definitely believe that to be true. However, my father has convinced himself that Whitefoot died of a broken heart, when, in fact, I believe it was a suicide. Had we not found him lying dead next to an empty bottle of Tylenol PM and what appeared to be the beginning stages of a suicide note, I would also have believed he died from sadness. I couldn't blame Whitefoot. The thought of spending the rest of my life alone with my father would drive me to take my own life too.

DAY #4/FATHER'S DAY

Somehow Dad managed to get ahold of a whistle. He uses it primarily for lifeguarding, and also to get the attention of anyone he wishes to have a conversation with. Today we were lying on the beach and I noticed that Dad can only balance his head midair while lying on his side. He was lying in that position for well over an hour. I asked, "Is that comfortable?" and he said, "It's perfectly fine." His head cannot touch the ground due to his inflamed abdomen. It just floats there, airborne.

Afterward, he said, "You are preternaturally genetically gifted, Chelsea. But, as far as your abs go, you could make some improvements." I wanted to ask him where his abs have been for the past forty years.

I'm really going to need some backup—all expenses paid.

Because it was Father's Day, I decided to change it up for dinner. Instead of going to our usual place, the four of us walked a quarter of a mile down the beach to another hotel and had dinner there.

We were seated next to a family with a six-year-old son who ran over to us and started dancing. Normally this would have been endearing, but this boy had an unusually large cranium and "crazy eyes." His pupils were extremely dilated and were two different sizes, not to mention they were each looking in completely opposite directions. As he hopped from one foot to the other, he jerked his head back and forth while making very disturbing grunting and hissing sounds. I couldn't make out where he was from; he wasn't using any actual words or a language, but his parents looked foreign. It was quite obvious that without severe behavioral modification, this boy would grow up to be a serial killer.

"Get that little fucker away from me," Shoniqua said, looking at him sideways.

My father took his eyes off the menu to look at the boy and lowered his reading glasses. "Boy's got dementia." Then, just as quickly, he returned to reading the menu.

The parents didn't seem to mind that their six-year-old was harassing another table, or think for a second we might not want to be entertained by their demon son.

The boy, let's call him Hitler, had a balloon in his hand and kept smacking it against his head while dancing. Luckily, Hitler had a crew cut that protected him from the static charge that this kind of action can create. I was not as lucky. It's not easy to discipline a child who is not related to you, so when he started rubbing the balloon against my head, I just sat there and let him do it, while my hair flew out in fifteen different directions.

"I'll have a margarita on the rocks, no salt," I said as Hitler continued to attack the side of my head with the balloon. The waitress, who looked apologetically at me but didn't speak much English, offered no support. Once my father ordered a margarita in Spanish, he put his menu down and finally noticed the kid accosting me. Shoniqua and Mama Latifa had noticed earlier and had been staring at the little boy with their mouths open.

"*¡Vamanos!*" my father said, putting his glasses in his shirt pocket.

"Don't yell at him," I said to my father. I felt bad for this boy, and although I don't particularly like getting hit in the head, I was grateful Hitler wasn't using a sharper object. He stopped hitting me with the balloon for a moment, but then seconds later picked up right where he left off.

"Why, Chels, are you enjoying it?" Mama Latifa asked me, grinning.

"Well, no, but obviously this boy doesn't have a particularly bright future ahead of him, and if this gives him some pleasure, then who am I to deny him?" I whispered. Why his parents weren't denying him this pleasure was another story. I looked over at their table and saw they were busy paying attention to their other two children, still oblivious to what was going on.

"Excuse me!" Mama Latifa yelled over to their table. "Can you come and get your fucking kid?"

The parents looked up, but didn't speak English. My father yelled something in Spanish that finally got their attention.

"This kid is like a wild dog. Did you ever see the movie *Cujo*?" he asked us as the mother came running over to our table.

"Dad, behave yourself. Do not insult this woman's son. Obviously, she knows he's got problems."

Hitler's mother came over and at first seemed apologetic, until my father berated her in what I later found out to be Portuguese. Soon her demeanor changed, and she grabbed her son by the arm and led him back to where they were eating, all the while giving Bitch Tits a death stare.

"Dad, what did you say? What is wrong with you?"

"What is wrong with *me*?" he asked. "Why do you have

to turn everything around? That boy's got dementia, Chelsea. Anyone can see that."

"Maybe he's fine," Shoniqua piped in. "Maybe his face is a mess because his mama whips his ass, because he doesn't know when to shut the fuck up."

"Amen," added Latifa, nodding.

"Amen," said Bitch Tits, and then high-fived Mama Latifa.

Then he raised his hand in the air and yelled, "I'd like the Chilean sea bass!" I turned to find our waiter was nowhere in sight, and realized the person Bitch Tits was ordering from was one of the hotel gardeners walking by, covered in dirt.

DAY #5

Today I woke up and looked outside to see Dad urinating on a tree. I looked across at Shoniqua's villa and saw her mother squatted by another tree doing the same thing. It's amazing how in sync these two are. It's 9 a.m. I just ordered marijuana from the groundskeeper.

DAY #5—20 MINUTES LATER

Things are really going downhill. I am begging any of you to come here. Shoniqua and her mother leave tomorrow. If left alone with this man for any period of time, I may take out a hit on him. I will not only pay for your ticket, I will also pay for you to bring a friend, a husband, a child, a stranger, whomever you'd like. I WILL ALSO THROW IN AN EXTRA $500 BONUS.

DAY #5—12 MINUTES LATER

Is it wrong for me to encourage Dad to swim when the riptide is at its strongest?

After the last e-mail home, my sister Sidney responded with an e-mail saying that she was on her way and would be arriving the next morning with her three kids. I really needed the backup since Shoniqua and Latifa were leaving in the morning. Moments later Isabel arrived with my pot. Things were looking up.

Shoniqua and her mother were packed and waiting for their taxi the next morning. I walked downstairs and found Mama Latifa and my father in a bear hug.

"All right, Papa Handler, you behave yourself," she said. "And thank you for everything."

"No problem," my father said. "It's my pleasure."

His pleasure? In no way, shape, or form had he contributed financially to this vacation. To be completely honest, I wasn't even sure my father had brought any money. If he had, he certainly wasn't spending it.

"Good-bye," I said, and hugged Shoniqua and her mama good-bye.

"Try and be patient with Papa Handler," Shoniqua said. "And Mama put her massage on your tab. Thanks."

"You hear that, Chelsea?" my father asked. "She's right. You need to respect your daddy."

"Thanks a lot," I said to Shoniqua as she leaned in for another hug.

"Good fucking luck," she said in my ear, and then started laughing hysterically as she headed toward her cab.

Bitch Tits put his arm around me as we watched the cab pull away and said, "Chels, I gotta be perfectly honest with you. What I'm really in the mood for is a good slice of pizza."

"Good luck with that," I replied, and headed back inside and upstairs to smoke my weed. Isabel had loaned me a pipe to smoke it in, and just as I took my first hit, I heard Shamu heading up the stairs.

"Chels, I'm not kidding about the pizza. All you have to do is get some dough, some tomato sauce, and some garlic."

"Dad, I don't know how to make a pizza. I can barely make eggs."

"What is that you got in your hand there?" he asked as I took another hit from the pipe. "Is that a peace pipe?"

"Yup," I told him. "I'm smoking the reefers."

"Well, that's a relief," he said. "Maybe they can help you relax a little. You're very uptight."

"Uptight" really isn't a word I think anyone would use to describe a girl who wrote a book documenting all of her one-night stands, but maybe my self-awareness needed a little sharpening. I was staring out at the ocean from the top floor of the open-aired villa, getting high with my father sitting next to me, when it occurred to me that this is what I needed all along. It had been a long time since I had gotten high and it was very strong weed. So instead of everything that came out of my dad's mouth annoying me to no end, it made me laugh hysterically. He also seemed a bit giggly, and I'm assuming he enjoyed a little second-hand highness.

My sister's taxi pulled up the next morning and I ran outside. I've never been so happy to see kids in all my life. I offered Sidney some pot the first night after dinner, and then she reminded me that she was a parent. But every day for the rest of our vacation, as soon as my dad smelled the reefer he came and sat by my side. These were the best of times.

Acknowledgments

I'd like to thank some people. Michael Broussard and his dog. Trish Boczkowski, Jennifer Bergstrom, and everyone at Simon Spotlight Entertainment. My family is very important, and even though you have very little to do with this book's coming to fruition, you have very much to do with this book's coming to fruition. Lastly, I'd like to thank Chuey. You are my nugget.

P.S. I'd also like to thank Regan Books for letting me out of my contract with them.

About the Author

Chelsea Handler is an accomplished stand-up comic and actress, as well as the bestselling author of *My Horizontal Life*. She is the star of her own late-night show on E!, *Chelsea Lately*; was one of the stars of *Girls Behaving Badly*; has appeared on *The Tonight Show with Jay Leno* and *Late Night with David Letterman*; and has starred in her own half-hour Comedy Central special. Chelsea makes regular appearances in comedy clubs across America and lives in Los Angeles.